View From the Edge of Over the Hill

To the 7 Lakes Library
From the Women's Club.

Margo Piper

Other Books From Margo Piper

Staying On Top

Jill Came Tumbling After

View From the Edge of Over the Hill

Reflections from Here

by
Margo Piper

RitAmelia Press

View from the Edge of Over the Hill: Reflections from Here
by Margo Piper
© 2000 by Margo Piper

Published by RitAmelia Press
7651 SE 118th Avenue
Morriston FL 32668-4843
(352) 465-4862

Printed in the United States of America

All rights reserved. No part of this book may be reproduced, stored in a retrieval system, or transmitted in any form or by any means, electronic, mechanical photocopying, recording or otherwise, without the prior written permission of the author.

ISBN: 0-9641216-5-4
Library of Congress Number Pending
Price: $9.95

Cataloging-in-Publication Data

Piper, Margo, 1916-
View from the Edge of Over the Hill: Reflections from Here/ by Margo Piper
    p. cm.
ISBN: 0-9641216-5-4
  1. Margo Piper, 1916- 2. Inspiration. 3. Motivation. 4. Caregiving. 5. Aging.
    I. Title
    CIP

Quotes that are not attributed are listed as anonymous in *Apples of Gold*, compiled by J. Petty (©1962, Gibson).

Dedication

To my dear Tony, who died April 3, 1999, on the 60th anniversary of our first date.

Contents

Preface	ix
Acknowledgments	x
Introduction. View From the Edge of Over the Hill	1
January 1. What is Important?	4
January 8. Communication Skills	6
January 15. Think Positive, Be Healthy!	9
January 22. Acceptance	11
January 29. How Do We Know We're Alive?	14
February 5. Midwinter Blues	16
February 12. Brain Power	18
February 19. How Do You Rate Your Day?	21
February 26. Hot Buttons	23
March 5. Relationships	25
March 12. Why Me?	28
March 19. Who's Okay?	30
March 26. Decisions	32
April 2. Smiles	35
April 9. Being Perfect	37
April 16. Night Owls	39

April 23. Growing Older Gracefully	41
April 30. Know What You Are Fighting For	43
May 7. Mother's Day	45
May 14. Wheel Balancing	47
May 21. Sharing Ourselves	49
May 28. The Spirit Has No Age	51
June 4. Nursing Home Phobia	53
June 11. Time Priorities	55
June 18. Staying On Top	57
June 25. Running in Place	59
July 2. Freedom	61
July 9. How Good Is Good?	63
July 16. Confident, Not Complacent	65
July 23. Alone or Lonely?	67
July 30. Others See Us	69
August 6. Know When to Say When	71
August 13. Obstacles	74
August 20. Who Are You?	76
August 27. Forgiveness	78
September 3. Hypochondria	80
September 10. Computer Gap	83
September 17. Posture	86
September 24. Take Advantage	88

October 1. Changing Others 90
October 8. Avoiding Accidents 92
October 15. Letting Go 94
October 22. Making Minutes Count 96
October 29. Nature's Way 99
November 5. Against the Tide 101
November 12. Self-Esteem 103
November 19. Stress 105
November 26. Right Questions/Right Answers 109
December 3. Packaging 110
December 10. Tackle Christmas Early 112
December 17. Share Your Memories 114
December 24. What Do We Tell Ourselves? 117
December 31. Re-examine Goals 120
Appendix A. Birthday Bonus. Extra Special 122
Appendix B. Special Observations for Caregivers
  A Reading for Spring 124
  A Reading for Summer 127
  A Reading for Autumn 129
  A Reading for Winter 132

Preface

Herein is a collection of essays written over the years, some of them having been published in other formats. Quite a few of them appeared in slightly different form in my first book, Staying on Top, while several others had their first incarnations in the monthly newsletters here at Shell Point. All have been updated and edited to make them more timely. Moreover, with a few more years under my belt, I was able to add more recent insights.

I hope the calendar format proves helpful in assisting readers find just the right sentiment for their needs. (And if you don't stick to the calendar precisely, who's to know?)

Acknowledgments

Singling out people for acknowledgment is always such a difficult job, because there are so many who have inspired and encouraged me in my writing. However, there are some to whom I wish to extend special thanks.

First and foremost, my editor, Drollene Brown, who kept after me until I got it together, then helped me get it together!

The Activities Staff here are Shell Point, who published many of my articles over the years, especially Dale, Tammy and Bianca.

My publicity agent, Paula, who managed to get me several interviews, both on TV and in the newspapers, plus lectures before various groups. It doesn't hurt to have people become familiar with your face.

My former employers at Weight Watchers of South Texas, in Houston. They taught me well the art of motivation, which will work for just about any subject one cares to pick. I try to practice what I preach, as well.

Bobbi Sims and her workshops opened my mind and taught me much about knowing myself.

The many friends who tell me my articles have helped them through difficult times. For that, I am most grateful. Helping others is just about the best thing we can do with our lives. If I can do this through my writing, I am content.

Introduction:
View From the Edge of Over the Hill

I WOULD HAVE TO BE IN PRETTY BAD SHAPE to admit being "over the hill"! On the other hand, simply surviving this long has put me on the edge of that hill, and it leaves me with some valuable experiences drawn from the pains and pleasures of living. That I am continuing to learn from all this endows me with a certain license to voice some of the conclusions I have reached.

Our children are not always interested in this wisdom, and I'm sure we were the same way. They want to draw their own conclusions from their own lives. That's one of the things I've been learning—when to bite my tongue when I see them heading for trouble. Sometimes our children do ask our advice, and that kind of dialogue is very rewarding.

This happens when our children learn to relate to us as people, not just parents. Their losing that feeling of childhood with us, finding us more like good friends, leads to many satisfying conversations. Some parents never get to this stage because of living far away and not seeing enough of the grown children to reach this happy transition. Their children may continue to carry some resentment about still feeling like kids when they're with the parents.

The best we can wish for our children is that they will be successfully independent, find work they love—be it gainful employment or raising a family—and someone with whom to share it. We read of many cases today in which grown children have had to ask to move home, due to lack of affordable housing or not being able to make it financially under the present economic conditions.

Few of us would refuse to help our children if we can accommodate them in a time of crisis. This requires some negotiation between parents and children. On the one hand, the parents have restructured their lives as the children grew up and moved out. The children, on the other hand, have had a taste of being on their own. They fear feeling like children in their parents' home again. It is likely to be a difficult transition for everyone concerned.

Working out balanced answers to the various questions of possible conflict are most important to harmony in this situation. Everyone must understand clearly his or her responsibilities, especially if grandchildren are involved. Being a grandparent has many wonderful advantages over being a parent. We can usually love unconditionally, without having the responsibilities of the daily disciplines. But when children move back home, babysitting tasks have to be pre-determined to the satisfaction and convenience of all.

Again, this involves dealing with each other on an adult-to-adult level. It is very rewarding when we really enjoy our adult children for themselves, and I'm sure there are times when they are surprised to feel the same way.

Those of us "on the edge" have much to offer, but it's important to share with those who want to listen! Didn't our mothers tell us: "Wait until you have children of your own"? Now we understand that message: eventually our children will understand!

"Our duty is to be useful, not according to our desires, but according to our powers."
—Ariel

January 1. What is Important?

WHAT IS IMPORTANT TO YOU? When you find the answer to that question, you will have a better idea of what you want to do with the rest of your life. What is your answer? Is it to take better care of yourself, to gain a better knowledge of your spirituality, to exercise more, to learn something new, to pursue a hobby long neglected, to learn to relax and enjoy your life more, to do more for others, to accept yourself?

I emphasize the importance of goals in one's life. We need long term goals as something to strive for, but we also need the small daily successes to keep us encouraged. Therefore, when we decide what is important to us, we can set about doing something constructive to achieve our goals. Before we start, it is necessary to know just where we are going.

You have the power to make positive changes in your life; success consists of *progress* toward your goals, not just reaching them. While you are sorting out your thoughts on the matter, you need to do some advance planning. Without definite steps to take, you may fall into a trap of using copouts to excuse or plan for failure. Many of us have experienced halfhearted goal setting. You goal has to be important enough to you to plan ahead how you will overcome the obstacles you are bound to encounter. It is imperative to be realistic with your expectations. You pretty well know what you can or will do, as well as what you can't (or *won't*) do. It won't help if you pick something you are unlikely to follow through on.

Believing in yourself is essential, but you aren't obliged to set monumental goals. Even small changes can make a big difference in your life. Take time to be truly thankful for what you have; where you are; your families, friends and neighbors; and all the beauty in your life. If you find there is more that you want from yourself, take time to think through what that is. What gives you pleasure? Include more such activities. If that means adjusting to some of the changes that have already occurred, what is your plan to move to more important things?

These questions are suggestions for you to start thinking of your own *important* things. Most of us are our own biggest obstacle, and we need to get out of our own way! Pick your goals and start thinking success, *today!*

*"The greatest distance
we have yet to cover
still lies within us."*

January 8. Communication Skills

RECENTLY I HAD A CONVERSATION with my about-to-be 18-year-old granddaughter, in which she bewailed her inability to communicate with her parents! Of course, I heard the same story from her parents' point of view. Most of us probably went through similar experiences in the process of growing up.

Good communication skills are much to be desired, and there are many helpful techniques we can use. First we must abandon the idea that certain people know us so well they should be able to read our minds! No matter how close we feel to someone, unless we share our thoughts verbally about the subject at hand, there is no way another person can know for sure how we feel about something. Can't we all remember times when we have muttered to ourselves that someone "should have known" how we felt?

An effective way to obtain a positive response when we want someone to understand how we feel is to consciously think and speak using the *I* message instead of *you*. Frame the way you feel by saying, "*I* feel sad (angry, disappointed, frustrated)" People can't really fault us for the way we feel about something, since that is something that just *is*. With such a message, we are less likely to put the other person on the defensive, because that is where a dialogue tends to break down. Everyone is interested in justifying his/her point of view. When we ask for their reaction to what we said, if they want to discuss it further, there is a chance for real understanding.

I have found enlisting the other person's cooperation in solving a mutual problem usually disarms the situation and eliminates the need to blame. The old saying, "You can catch more flies with honey than vinegar," works quite well in most cases. There will be times when these techniques seem too threatening to the other person to respond; however, staying with how you feel can sometimes help the other individual react more willingly and can open new doors of communication.

If you find yourself in a circumstance in which you believe there will never be any communication, express what you can say comfortably and try to avoid that situation in the future. There are people who feel anxious when they are asked how they feel about something because they don't even have the vocabulary to describe the emotion. They may have trouble sustaining relationships because they tend to deal only with surface feelings; they fear going deeper. We often hesitate to reveal our true selves when we are uneasy about what that true self may be.

You may be surprised to find that when you risk expressing how you feel, others will feel more at ease about revealing their feelings. You have a right to express yourself as long as you don't hurt others or yourself. Learning to know when to give vent to your feelings and when not to, is the wisdom we seek.

"The kindly word that falls today may bear its fruit tomorrow."

January 15. Think Positive, Be Healthy!

THE BENEFICIAL LINK BETWEEN POSITIVE THINKING and the quality of our lives is something I've spoken of and written about over the years. Now there appears to be evidence that our attitude can have a positive effect on our immune system!

Medical science has been studying patients with terminal diseases who have made remarkable spontaneous recoveries. Patients whose cancers proved inoperable were just sewn up and informed that nothing else could be done except to keep them comfortable. For whatever reason, the surgeon later found all evidence of the cancer had disappeared! Was it exposure to the air? There were simply no logical solutions.

Dr. Bernie Siegel, in his book, *Love, Medicine and Miracles*, reported his study of many cases of miraculous cures. There seemed to be a definite connection between the patient's attitude about his condition and the actual improvement in his immune system. Scientific tests bore this out. Patients who refuse to give in to their illness can often change the immune system in measurable ways sufficiently to effect cures or, at the least, improve the quality of their remaining days. The immune system can be monitored by tests that show the actual increase in disease-fighting cells.

Science is only now finding out about the power

of our minds and the fact that we have a lot more control over that power than we ever imagined. The connection between body and mind is proving to be very exciting research material. There is a Mind/Body Clinic now that teaches people how to tap into that power through the "Relaxation Response." This scares some people, but it need not. To use this technique, one simply learns to clear the mind of negative thoughts and get in touch with one's own *Inner Wisdom*. When we take time to be still, we can often see pathways not previously apparent to us.

Making positive affirmations of our worth, wisdom, patience and outlook when we feel overwhelmed by circumstances can do much to build our self-esteem. Further, we can recognize the power of thinking positively. This encourages us to live with love and joy and in the *now*. If we manage to do this, our bodies will respond in ways we can't see. It will help us become more resistant to disease, as well as stronger and wiser. As Eugene Vodev says: "The mind/body philosophy is best expressed very simply: "View the body as a temple, not just as something to apply remedies to, but to nurture from the inside out'."

"What counts is not the number of hours you put in, but how much you put into the hours."

January 22. Acceptance

ACCEPTANCE IS SOMETHING WE HAVE HEARD ABOUT most of our lives. Accepting ourselves, however, is often a lot easier said than done. No one wants us to lie down and give up hope, but accepting the toll that aging or disease takes on our bodies or accepting the loss of a loved one is the first step to healing the loss. If we continue to be angry inside at our present circumstances, it is almost impossible to think positively about what options are still available to us. To quote Dr. Norman Vincent Peale: "Don't settle for your limitations"!

We can "go through a change, or *grow* through a change." Quality of life depends more on growth than getting older. The ageless people I remember best, and have admired, all have one thing in common: an enthusiasm for life. Losing a loved one or losing abilities on which we have come to depend must be properly mourned and eventually accepted.

Perhaps you do not agree that these two categories have that much in common. However, as with any loss, it is essential for good mental and physical health to reach the decision to let go and accept the new circumstances.

Perhaps you have already found how true the words are to the song, "The Way We Were." We tend to forget the unhappy events and remember the laughter when there has been a loss. If we give our mind a chance, it will help us heal and accept. The pain of a loss will not go away, nor would we want it to, but time does enable us to "remember the laughter" and go on from there.

There are ways to help yourself do this. Think about starting a new activity. Learning something new can be exhilarating, and this is where some of us can possibly reclaim some of our old enthusiasm. Perhaps relaxing and letting go, in order to enjoy the benefits of a less-hurried life, will be the answer for others. If we can learn to release our frustration, anger, fear, anxieties and worries through prayer, meditation or introspection, we will find greater peace and courage to *grow* in a different direction, through acceptance.

Reach out to others in need of comfort or support. There is nothing like doing for others to take yourself out of yourself. If your profession, hobby or interests have blessed you with unusual experiences, share them by writing them down. If this is impossible, learn to use a tape recorder. Make notes to go by and after a little practice, you will find it no big thing to talk to a machine. Remember how we hated answering machines at first? (Maybe you still do.) Now, however, most of us think little about leaving messages.

You can become used to a tape recorder in the same way. This method of passing your experiences and wisdom along allows the message to be heard in your own words, in your own voice, so the listeners can hear how you actually sounded. A step beyond this is the new camcorder, which enables the present generation to maintain a moving, speaking record of themselves. I have heard of wills being recorded on videotape so there would be no doubts about what the person had in mind. Perhaps the videotapes can help solve the distressing problems often experienced with wills and trusts after a death. In whatever form you use, as you communicate about your past and the way you feel, you learn to accept yourself.

However you go about achieving acceptance, you will gradually acquire peace of mind. Still, you will agree with the oft repeated adage: "Growing old is not for sissies!"

*"To be content with little is difficult.
To be content with much, impossible."*

January 29. How Do We Know We're Alive?

WITH PRESENT MEDICAL TECHNOLOGY, even professionals are not as sure as they used to be that they know the answer to that question. In most cases, we know we are alive by the fact that our heart is beating and we are breathing under our own power.

Is it living to simply be alive? When we are *living*, we continue to learn and grow. Each day is new and brings opportunity. If we are *living*, we do not stand still! We are unique and have varied goals and ambitions. There are those who avoid challenges, for in their reasoning, it is safer to avoid risking failure. Some believe this can insulate us from pain, but it can also keep us from experiencing *living*.

We find many substitutes for the things we feel are missing and due us in our lives: sleeping or eating too much; hiding in our comfortable nests (literally or figuratively), rather than taking on what each new day has to offer. Maybe you fall into the category of rationalizing that there is not much life can offer you any more. In reality, however, you have as much time today as you have ever had. Forgive yourself for fancied or real errors of the past; accept your disappointments; then see what you can do with what presents itself today.

Most of our accomplishments are not spur of the

moment, but involve some advance planning. I am a great list-maker, since I discovered a long time ago that was the only way I could keep track of things. I no longer set deadlines for myself, but there is great satisfaction when I can cross off completed tasks.

You can't count on others to get you to start *living*, but there are exceptions of good friends or doctors who may give you a good nudge now and then. Most of us end up about as happy as we decide to be.

Changing one's attitudes or actions can be challenging. We have to believe the ad: "I'm worth it!" It's more than a cliché. Take it one day at a time and make it a day for living, loving and learning.

> *"Try to fix the mistakes,*
> *not the blame."*

February 5. Midwinter Blues

WHAT DO YOU THINK OF YOUR ABILITY TO COPE? Do you have a positive attitude about your capabilities? Do you feel confident that you can manage the situations life hands you?

Let us consider attitudes and what we can do differently when we find ourselves operating in a negative gear. (It happens to all of us from time to time.) February is noted as a period when people feel down. This is given scientific credence by the valid medical theory that in northern latitudes the absence of enough exposure to sunlight can bring on the "blues." Although we can't use that excuse in southern climes, a post-holiday letdown, before spring arrives, can account for the feelings.

Post–holiday depression can be due to outside events: a recent move, illness, inability to do things physically the way you used to, the fact that family and good friends live far away and are unable to be with you. There is a lot of good advice in all the publications before the holidays, and you may feel pleased with the ways you coped. Thinking back, maybe you didn't do as well as you thought. Perhaps you need to review your expectations and attitudes. The holidays are long gone, but do you have a "long gone" feeling left over after all the festivities? There are a couple of tried and true methods to get cheerful again and back on track.

Reach out in your present relationships to improve the quality or quantity of those friendships. Don't be afraid to make the first move. Look to people you would like to know better and see what you can do to get something going. Someone has to start; you may as well be the one. Do something for someone less fortunate; this really can take you out of yourself. Give without thought of return, simply for the need of giving.

You can change the quality of your life and relationships by changing whether you look at problems as opportunities or obstacles. "Can't" often means "won't," which we can decide to change to "will."

"Happiness is not dependent on circumstances, but on our reaction to them."

February 12. Brain Power

SCIENTISTS ARE NOW ABLE TO OBSERVE people's brains without surgery! From a medical article on that subject, I learned that they are beginning to understand how our brains work by using new imaging techniques. With the various types of scanning machines now available, they are able to pinpoint what part of the brain is affected by emotion, stress, drugs, physical activity and mental activity. Through other improved methods of testing, they have found that our brains do not necessarily stop growing as we age! By examining different types of brain cells, they conclude that active seniors' brains continue to grow and develop new brain cells. The toll of disease or injury in people of all ages is also under investigation.

It should encourage us to know that when we exercise our minds the way we do our bodies, the cells continue to grow and expand as they have been doing since before we were born. The key seems to be to keep ourselves challenged mentally. One of my favorite suggestions is to plan many pleasurable activities in our lives. These keep us alert, interested and interesting, and in turn, stimulate our minds. If our challenge is something we enjoy, it is more likely we will pursue this activity. As with most goals, they have to be *our* goals in order to motivate us.

It is good to know we don't have to sit around and wait for our brains to deteriorate. Disease or injury can do this, but it doesn't "just happen" to most of us. When we contemplate how little of the total brain is used by even the geniuses of the world, we realize there is a lot up there to work with. The outlook is exciting for research on some of our most distressing diseases affecting brain function: Alzheimer's, Parkinson's, strokes and other malfunctions.

New information indicates that, by refusing to do nothing but sit in our rocking chairs, we have a lot of control over the way our brain continues to operate. We can start thinking of subjects we have always wanted to know more about. Many of us have more time to give to such projects now.

Stimulating and informative books are readily available, and exciting and educational tapes bring subjects right into our homes. If we are fortunate enough to have access to a computer, opportunities are endless. Courses offer other options, sometimes at no or very little cost for those wanting more instruction. Often, retired people turn out to be excellent students since we are taking these courses because we want to.

Learning new crafts or hobbies gives us the satisfaction of mastering a new skill.

Another avenue is volunteer work. Doing for others has lots of side effects on the giver—good ones! Barring disease or injury, most of us can keep chugging along and grow new synapses in our brains. (This is the way our brain talks to itself.)

Keeping a balance in our emotional, spiritual, physical, intellectual, social and material goals is essential for good mental health. It's reassuring to know:

"The old gray matter just keeps rolling along."
(Apologies from the author to "Old Man River!")

February 19. How Do You Rate Your Day?

IF YOU RATED THE ACTIVITIES OF EACH DAY from one to ten, according to how much enjoyment you got out of each one, how many activities would get a ten, or even a nine or eight? How much time do you spend doing things you really like to do?

Modern research indicates that those of us who spend more time doing things we enjoy are healthier and have more energy. A proposed college course for retired couples was given to me for evaluation. One assignment was to document any improvement in attitude or well-being by consciously scheduling more pleasurable activities each day. I thought about my own schedule, and I started charting to see how many pleasurable activities I could count in my days on a scale of one to ten.

Sometimes we find our routine doesn't include enough activities we can rate with a high number. This can lead us, at the very least, to low energy and boredom or, worse, depression. I believe both men and women today are more aware of doing things that will improve their lives and health and reduce stress. We are finding that sensible eating, exercise, and enjoyable activities all contribute to the quality of our lives.

Perhaps some of your favorite activities have to be curtailed or given up altogether for health reasons. How do you feel when you have to give up and let go of something you have previously enjoyed? Letting go and accepting a loss, any loss, involves going through the grief process: denial, anger, grief and bargaining. Acceptance means acknowledging that a change has taken place; it is up to you to take action. Although the grief is still there, you must find other goals and new activities that will bring you pleasure.

Make a list of twenty things you love to do. This can include very simple pleasures, such as listening to music or talking books, taking a soaking bath, reading, writing, watching TV, calling on a friend, doing something for someone. More ambitious activities can be listed, too.

Check the balance in your life regarding the spiritual, emotional, social, physical, intellectual and nutritional patterns. All these parts must be in accord. How is yours *now*?

> "The secret of happy living is not
> to do what you like,
> but to like what you do."
> —From author's files

February 26. Hot Buttons

WE ALL HAVE HOT BUTTONS, and most of us know very well who and what pushes those annoying buttons. Think about the situations in your life that you can, with certainty, predict will push those buttons—occasions when you know you will find yourself *reacting* rather than *acting*.

It may be something like road rage, or a thoughtless remark from someone who is important to you. Maybe it is experiencing interference with plans carefully made. You then feel guilty because you *shouldn't* let such things get to you. But shoulds don't count, because you know the feelings are there anyway. What you must do is recognize that feelings are neither good nor bad; they just *are*. What counts is the action you take as a result of such feelings.

For instance, when I am tired, that is when I find my hot buttons being pushed. I am also one of those people who is not very awake until I've had my breakfast. I generally advise my near-and-dear to let me wake up properly before any substantive conversation. I know I have company on that one!

Becoming aware of your own push button behavior can help you start thinking of new ways to deal with your formerly predictable reactions. When you recognize that one of your buttons has been pushed, a good start is to take a deep breath and relax. Most push button behaviors come when you tense up in certain situations you can see coming. Counting to ten still works! It gives you time to take control and change your usual reaction. Once you become aware of your problem areas, you are well on the way to finding solutions. As with other problems, recognition removes most of the stress, and it's easier to let it go consciously.

Maintaining a sense of humor when you recognize a familiar reaction can help diffuse things. When there are interpersonal relationships involved, wait to discuss the situation until emotions won't get in the way. When you get emotional, your reason is not in gear. If the other person gets defensive, no one is listening to anyone! Using the *I* message—"I feel ____ because . . ." or "I wish (or I'd rather) you ____"— puts everyone on the same level. That is a good starting place. Press *Delete*!

"Those who cannot remember the pain of the past, are doomed to repeat it."

March 5. Relationships

Have you felt you could get along with most people well, then have that belief challenged when you run into someone who appears to be hostile for reasons unknown to you?

If this is a family member or someone with whom you have to work, this becomes upsetting and can become an extremely stressful situation. We recognize stress as our feeling frustrated, hurt, angry, afraid or helpless. We feel it as a lack of control in some part of our lives. Is it possible to get someone else to change? Unless they want to change, it is impossible. Haven't you experienced times when someone wanted you to change, perhaps to give up a bad habit or lose weight? Unless these were your goals as well, you wished they would get off your case. The only person anyone has real power to change is himself.

When you change the way you approach a personality conflict, it helps not to inflict your expectations on the situation. This way the other person is less likely to react defensively. Eventually, you may be able to deal with each other on an equal basis, thereby diminishing the conflict.

On the other hand, there will be times when the person with whom you are in conflict is not willing to give an inch as far as you are concerned, no matter how hard you try. Sometimes this is hard to accept, and you keep looking for solutions longer than is productive. Even though positive recognition normally reinforces positive behavior (reward), some situations require more doing than others. Still, if you persevere, you may find the situation improving as you concentrate on looking for positives. Eventually you may be more successful than you had hoped.

The wrongs that keep you from trying to improve a relationship may be real or fancied. If you believe you are "in the right," you may not be anxious to take the first step in mending the rift. Being willing to go first will often remove enough pressure to resolve the misunderstanding.

Standing up for your rights without rancor or emotion works much better when you do not force the other person to be defensive. This is certainly better than feeling you let others walk all over you! This technique works as well in secondary relationships (with people who are not personal acquaintances). If I know I am going to return an item to a store and complain about poor service or a broken promise, I will plan a script in my mind or on paper. This way, I can be sure to say what I want to say, the way I want to say it.

Communicating on an equal basis without letting emotions get in the way will enable both parties to handle the situation more constructively. At times, when appropriate, I will write my thoughts in a letter. The advantage of this is that I can make my point dispassionately without being interrupted. It may be "chicken," but it works well.

In all types of interpersonal relationship

problems, we can see how changing the way we think and act instead of expecting everyone else to do the changing can work positively for all parties concerned. Even if we get nowhere with our positive attitude, dealing with others on an equal basis will usually make for more pleasant associations.

"Be what you wish others to become."

March 12. Why Me?

LIFE IS A RISKY BUSINESS, and sometimes we feel we are getting more than our share of knocks. It is tempting to ask, "Why me?" and brood about the situation with less than optimism.

When we think about it, most of the time our lives sail along on a fairly even keel, and we tend to forget that life itself is a challenge. We are obliged to face it every day, and how we face it reveals our attitude toward it.

Were you ever told to "Keep a stiff upper lip?" There is a lot to be said for that attitude, since it avoids getting into the "poor me" routine. Every challenge you go through adds to your growth as a human being, There is much comfort when you feel you have weathered adversity well. Maintaining that positive attitude throughout can actually make you and others feel better. In practice, this is many times easier said than done, but it is well worth the effort.

If you practice living in the *now,* with anticipation and appreciation of what each moment holds, there will probably not be as many roller coaster highs and lows. You will more likely be able to accept what *is* and deal with each moment as it develops, whether positive or negative in your eyes.

Your attitude about your circumstances can be a way to prove that you can manage to survive the worst and feel satisfied about the way you handled the situation. Challenges you have overcome make you much stronger for further adversity.

Living each moment of your life by appreciating the good times and doing the best you can with the bad, is really all that is asked of you.

Remember the song: "Pick yourself up, dust yourself off, and start all over again!" This can inspire you to hang on the next time you feel things caving in on you.

> *"It takes as much energy*
> *to be unhappy*
> *as to be happy.*
> *How will you spend your energy?"*
> —John Bradshaw

March 19. Who's Okay?

How would you describe yourself? Aggressive? Assertive? Non-assertive (passive)? Do you understand the differences? An aggressive person is one who says or implies, "I'm okay but you are not!" A non-assertive or passive person, on the other hand, is likely to say or imply, "You are okay, but I am not okay!" An assertive person says or implies, "I'm okay and you're okay. Let's talk."

An aggressive person is likely to feel he is always right, that it's the other person's fault when things go wrong. A non-assertive person is always willing to accept that it is probably his fault. These are the guilt-carriers.

The assertive person is willing to accept differences of opinion and is anxious to discuss solutions. He learns how to achieve his objectives by talking about how he feels about a situation, rather than challenging or accusing the other person. When someone tells us how we should have done something or that we messed up, don't we immediately get defensive and try to justify ourselves? If, on the other hand, someone tells us how he felt and we really listen to the words, we can see we are not threatened by such statements since we are not being accused. In this way, a dialogue can be initiated and solutions sought.

When we are in a situation that upsets us, if we

speak in those terms instead of complaining or criticizing, the discussion process is likely to become more productive. We can enlist the other person's aid in finding solutions.

An additional assertive technique is to always make requests rather than demands, using the "I wish you would ___" and "I'd rather you would ___" to explain your rationale. When you try this technique, you'll be amazed at how well it can work. Since there is no right or wrong with feelings, the actions you take or request will make the difference. You might make a new friend or reinforce an old relationship. You can't have too many of either of these!

"We are all manufacturers, making goods, making troubles or making excuses."

March 26. Decisions

THERE AREN'T MANY OF US who haven't had to face making hard decisions. The usual advice is to make a list of all the pros and cons, thereby clarifying the situation. A list will help, both when the options aren't obvious and when there are many options.

In a recent monumental house cleaning of my files, I ran across many long-forgotten treasures I had collected, among which was an article on making decisions. It offered more than just the pros and cons, so I believe it is worth passing on.

When one feels unable to make a particular decision, it helps to write down all the particulars. I have found writing down answers to questions I am asking myself to be a helpful exercise. It enables me to zero in on just what decisions are involved, as well as what options I have to consider.

When you have tried to make some sort of decision with no progress, try putting the dilemma on paper. A first step is to decide what it is you want from this decision and what brought you to the place where you had to make it. Write down all you can about the present situation and how you feel about it. When you see your thinking written down, it can have a calming effect, just as taking action in any difficult situation can make you feel as though you are more in control again. It is that helpless, hopeless feeling—that lack of control—that brings us up against a wall, making it hard to think creatively.

When you have written down all possibilities, there may be some new, unexpected option that will occur to you. Of course it is possible that there is only one option, and you may not like it much. As long as there is only one possible way to go, there is no decision to make. If there is no solution, there is no problem. Have you figured it out? How many times do you waste time and thought, getting stressed out, when there isn't really any more you can do? Don't forget prayer. Often being quiet and relaxed will allow you to come up with wiser decisions.

Imagine that your goal is behind you. What are the most important things that will make a difference in how you are feeling now and when it is all behind you? Since the only person you have the power to change is yourself, does your solution involve another person's changing? If so, what can you do to change your own attitude, to start you on a productive train of thought? Once you change your approach, other avenues will appear. Now that you have clarified both the decision and your own attitude, what other things will affect your choices? What actually needs to be confronted and what can you throw out as unacceptable or unrealistic?

Many times, we hope circumstances will cause others to make the decision for us, but do we want to give control over our lives to someone else, as well as handing them the blame or the credit for the success or failure of our solution? If this is unavoidable, *that* may be the choice we have to face.

Pray over it and make an informed decision using all the tools that will get you there. If you can conceive a solution, you can achieve it. Once you determine the proper course of action, go for it!

"The real art of life consists in finding out what is the question to be solved, and the person who can find out what problem is to be solved, is the man who really makes contributions to Life."
—Abbott Lawrence Lowell

April 2. Smiles

*"The world is like a mirror,
reflecting what you do,
and if you face it smiling,
it smiles right back at you."*

HAVEN'T WE ALL KNOWN PEOPLE who go around looking like they carry the weight of the world? Along with that, they usually expect the worst to happen, and it often does!

On the other hand, there are the eternal optimists who are sure things will somehow turn out right. Their whole personality radiates confidence and joy. Perhaps it has to do with a strong religious faith, but there is always a great difference in their outlook on life. In a course I once took, an assignment involved looking for good in everyone throughout the week. It was most interesting hearing about the positive experiences of the class. Most of us were surprised to find good in unexpected places when we took the time and trouble to look for it.

This has to do with recognizing the good in ourselves, as well. It does include being realistic about our strengths, goals and abilities, and it includes accepting ourselves, totally. We can help ourselves do this by repeating good, positive thoughts about who and what we are many times during our day.

Accepting responsibility for our thoughts as well as our actions is also important. We may not always believe we can control our thoughts, but we can resolve to push negative ones out of our minds, by replacing them with our mental list of happy, positive thoughts. The serenity of our acceptance of ourselves will be reflected to all whom we meet.

Many of us find it difficult to think of ourselves in a favorable light. Part of this may come from being admonished as a child not to be conceited. We tend to feel faintly guilty when we are pleased with ourselves. It may take some practice to think of ourselves as capable, confident people if we are used to believing such behavior is immodest. We are more likely to dwell on our self-perceived shortcomings. There should be joy in knowing we have done a job well. Too often, there is no pride in doing good work these days.

Discover how a smile from the heart reflects back to you from those you meet. A smile speaks of a loving acceptance of yourself and others. This is your mission.

> "It is not easy to find happiness in ourselves, and it is not possible to find it elsewhere."
> —Agnes Repplier

April 9. Being Perfect

ARE THERE ANY PERFECTIONISTS OUT THERE? There is a little bit in most of us, but some of us have a great big dose of "Be Perfect!" to deal with. Perfection is not only impossible, but trying to be so may be counterproductive. As you strive to be the perfect partner, wife, husband, dieter, non-smoker, non-drinker, you may develop tendencies that could be hazardous to your health.

For one thing, you may view your goals in "all or none" categories by seeing and emphasizing only your failures, not your successes. Do you see aspects of your life in a black or white fashion? You are either on or off the wagon, in or out of love, a smoker or a non-smoker, on or off your diet! There is no middle ground, no gray area.

If you think back to the clichés you heard as a child, you can see where many of these ideas came from: "Anything worth doing, is worth doing well!" "Always do your best!" "You can do better!" When perfection is your goal, one error brings failure!

You need to take it a little easier on yourself, realizing that change, even positive change, can be stressful. Even changes that are welcome put more demands on your personal resources. You can learn to cope even though you don't achieve perfection.

Your self-doubt will be most apparent when you are considering a plan for change that will require some effort on your part. This will also be present while you are in the process of executing that change. These are times when you need to realize it is natural to have doubt when you are experiencing difficulties. If, in addition, you start with unrealistic goals, you can easily talk yourself into defeat and giving up.

Small successes are the key to overcoming the self-doubts. Give yourself permission to be less than perfect and still be okay and on track. Evaluate your progress from the starting point, not from the destination. Take it one step at a time and do what you can do *now*.

> "Besides the noble art of getting things done. There is the art of leaving things undone. The wisdom of life consists in the elimination of non-essentials."
>
> —Lin Yutang

April 16. Night Owls

Nights when I was wakeful, I looked around the neighborhood and wondered what the other "night owls," whose lights I could see, were doing or thinking. This happened to be when I did a lot of my writing, but it was not always that way.

I discovered in my last couple of years of high school that I was a night person. When I found that my work progressed better late at night, I structured my studying accordingly. Most of us recognize fairly early in life if we are *day* or *night* people; there is a physiological reason for this. It is our circadian rhythm, our internal clock, that determines when we feel alert or sleepy. It also affects mental and emotional processes during the approximate 24-hour period. It is possible to change our body rhythms. For the best results, it should be done gradually, adjusting the schedule one way or the other a little at a time. When we have "jet lag," our circadian rhythm has been disturbed. Studies have found it is easier to adjust forward rather than back.

Some time ago I found there were nights when I didn't get to sleep until 3:30 or 4:00 A.M. It was happening as often as once or twice weekly. I was amazed when I felt fairly normal the next day after only three or four hours of sleep! I usually conked out the next night and caught up. Nevertheless, I found it very frustrating and boring, lying there perhaps most of the night, very unhappy that I wasn't sleeping. When I consulted my doctor eventually, she suggested I use the time to read, write or do chores, whatever struck my fancy. I was skeptical, but it turned out to be a very productive solution. There is still that part of me that says it can't be good for me to do without sleep, but facts point to the opposite conclusion. Many of us don't require as much sleep when we get older, but others need more.

If you get into a period of wakefulness, there are steps you can take to improve your sleep habits. It is better if you give yourself a half to one hour to fall asleep. When it doesn't happen, you can get up and do something that won't stimulate you too much, such as reading or writing. Cutting out the consumption of caffeine beverages after 4:00 P.M. may be beneficial. Some find taking a short walk in the evening helps; for others, this proves too stimulating. It takes some experimenting to see what works for you. Perhaps a soaking bath or shower will enable you to unwind. For some, soothing music helps to achieve a relaxed feeling.

If you find you are suffering ill effects from lack of sleep, be sure to check with your doctor. However, you may find you can get along with less sleep. Perhaps you can plan to stay up later or get up earlier. After allowing a reasonable time to fall asleep at night, get up. You may accomplish some unexpected things when you are wakeful. Use this time as a gift. Don't fight it, use it!

"The rest of our days depends on the rest of our nights."

April 23. Growing Older Gracefully

THE HUSBAND OF A FRIEND ONCE SAID: "If you have *it* when you are young, you will always have *it!*"

What is *it*? *It* is what makes us notice one person over another. Overall appearance (not necessarily beauty) will usually be the first thing we notice about someone new. A person with *it* will probably be well groomed and suitably dressed, will have sparkle, enthusiasm and a pleasant expression. It will be obvious that this person takes good care of himself or herself. Growing awareness these days of the importance of physical fitness and good nutrition makes us pay more attention to these qualities.

You are probably aware of all the "walkers" these days, in addition to those who regularly attend exercise classes, both in the gym and in the pool. If you are unable to participate in active exercise, do not despair. Maintaining a youthful outlook and a lively interest in life, other people and current events and continuing to learn and live each day will give you that sparkle and enthusiasm that knows no age.

If you agree this is important, you may ask, "How do I get IT . . . or keep IT? Think back to the times of your life when you had the most fun. For me, it was when I was learning something new I really enjoyed. In a learning situation, everything is new and exciting; we need to keep this feeling alive, retain that excitement for living.

Cultivating enthusiasm for everything you do can help you have that sparkling mind and radiant glow and let everyone you meet know you are alive and vigorous.

Ralph Waldo Emerson said: "Nothing great was ever achieved without enthusiasm." Think about that. Perhaps "adequate" or even "pretty good" can be achieved without enthusiasm, but not "great." We are all salesmen in a sense, selling ourselves, and we need enthusiasm for our product.

Your attitude can determine your enthusiasm. How many times have you talked yourself into a state over a trifle? Attitudes are learned; they can also be unlearned. *Act* enthusiastic and you will *become* enthusiastic. Be aware just from living as long as you have that you are bound to have picked up a lot of good knowledge that can help you handle your life effectively.

To grow older gracefully, maintain a zest for living, look for the good in everyone, be optimistic and smile. Good things will just naturally happen!

*"So long as enthusiasm lasts,
so long is youth still with us."*

April 30. Know What You Are Fighting For

It is probable that many of us at this point are in one stage or another of fighting or accepting some conditions of our aging. To many of us, the fact that we are sometimes written off because of our age makes mention of our "being old" fighting words. We don't like to be lumped into that category!

It can be a good thing to keep fighting, but let's be sure what we need to fight for. Acceptance of the way we are at this point in life is necessary before any fight can begin. So often we lose precious time fighting things we have no power to change. Once we are able to accept the facts of our life, we can begin to plan to make the most of life from now on . . . with a higher possibility of success. This way, we are fighting *for* something instead of *against* something.

Facing a personal health crisis that left me with chronic fatigue, I found I was exceedingly and frighteningly angry that this happened to me. I recall that, from a very early age, I believed anger was an unacceptable emotion in our house. I took pride in the fact that I didn't get angry often. As I evaluated the way I felt about my illness, I realized I had now become angry at God and was waiting for lightening to strike for even thinking such thoughts!

Many of us grow up thinking it's unacceptable to express anger, and we manage to stuff down such thoughts over the years. When a crisis occurs, we finally realize what we have been doing. Of course I had gotten angry in the past! I just didn't let anyone know.

It is important to reestablish our relationship with God, haul out the old and new anger, recognize it, resolve it and let it go. I had a lot of letting go to do! It is only when we learn to do this that acceptance is finally achieved. An added benefit: you may find your sense of humor has returned. Allowing anger to go unrecognized and unresolved can cause you to forget laughter.

Once you are over that hump, you will find it much easier to sort out what you can do with your life from here on. That doesn't guarantee you won't have problems dealing with acceptance; that challenge comes and goes. However, it finally sinks in that you can stop using up your available energy to try to find the magic that will make you feel the way you did when you were younger. A fight to get back to what you think you always were takes energy away from what you must face and accept. As trite as it sounds, learning to live each day as joyfully as possible will do much to compensate for the time you have lost, the years you spent nurturing inner anger.

Relax. Let go and open new doors! Face and deal with the new reality and put what you still have to good use, putting aside mourning what used to be.

"You can't get anywhere today if you are still mired down in yesterday."

May 7. Mother's Day

A GOOD WAY TO FOLLOW UP ON MOTHER'S DAY is to include a walk down memory lane, remembering the sayings she used to repeat frequently when you were growing up. Mothers seem to be in sync on these admonitions. I'm certain many of us have used the same ones on our children and grandchildren.
- You can do it if you really want to.
- If you can't be good, be careful.
- Stand up straight!
- That's as crooked as a dog's hind leg!
- If something gets to be too hard to do, we aren't meant to do it.
- Keep your hands away from your face!
- Never stack your dishes at the table.
- Keep your elbows off the table.
- Always wear clean underwear, you might be in an accident!
- Someday, you'll thank me for this!
- Wait until you have children of your own!
- If you can't say something good, don't say anything.
- Don't dwell on negative thoughts.
- Handsome is as handsome does.
- You can't tell a book by its cover.
- Don't forget your gloves.
- Mind your manners.

- Stand up when being introduced and when an older person enters the room.
- Mind your Ps and Qs. (Anyone know what Ps and Qs are?)
- It's better to be safe than sorry.
- This, too, shall pass.
- Use your head to save your heels.
- If it's to be, it's up to me.
- Wash hands before eating, and after using the bathroom.
- Look both ways before crossing the street.
- Come straight home.
- Never talk to strangers.
- Your E is bigger than your B. (Your eyes are bigger than your belly.)
- What the eyes don't see, the heart doesn't cry for.
- Many a mickle makes a muckle.
- Watch out what you wish for, you might get it!
- Eat your crusts, they will make your hair curl.
- Never promise what you can't deliver.
- The more haste, the less speed.
- You can catch more flies with honey than vinegar.
- About gossip. Think: Is it kind? Is it true?
- Would you like it said about you?

"Fine eloquence consists in saying all that should be, not all that could be said."

May 14. Wheel Balancing

As we grow older we may feel there aren't many goals for us to set anymore. We are going to enjoy our friends and families, keep on top of our expenses, appreciate the natural beauty that surrounds us, so why bother with goal setting? Let's test that theory.

For a satisfying life, you have to feel that all the facets of your life are in balance. Think of these aspects as your life's wheel spokes: spiritual, physical, emotional, material, intellectual and charitable. If some are too short or too long, your wheel will not turn smoothly. It might be helpful to list the goals connected with each one, and on a scale of one to ten, decide if you have achieved balance in this category. If you haven't, plan how to bring them more in line. Be specific, since "vague goals yield vague results."

There is always room to set both short- and long-term goals for yourself, no matter where you stand at any given moment. When you have set goals that seem unreachable, you give up before you try. This is where the short-term goal comes in. You must be *very* confident you will be able to reach it, for success breeds success. When you reach a short-term goal, it is time to embark on the next small step, and don't forget to pat yourself on the back for the victory. If you don't set goals, you will drift, with no destination in mind.

Your goals must not depend on someone else's doing something differently. You know you can change only yourself. By changing *your attitude*, you can often accomplish the change you seek in others. It is so beautiful to discover this. You may have been banging your head against a brick wall for ages, with resulting stress for both parties. When you relax and stop trying to control others, lo and behold, sometimes the change just happens when the pressure is off! This also cuts down the tension for both parties, which may be why it works so well.

Ponder these aspects of your life and set new goals in the categories you feel need something more for balance. Resolve to be a more balanced, joyous person.

"Do not be angry that you cannot make others as you wish them to be, since you cannot make yourself as you wish to be."
—Thomas A. Kempis

May 21. Sharing Ourselves

My book *Jill Came Tumbling After*, which was edited from journals I had been keeping since the onset of my husband's memory loss, shared my experiences and feelings. I found it allowed others to share similar thoughts from their lives. Caregivers can put up a very good front, and most of us don't reveal even to our near-and-dear all that is happening to us, even though our world is falling apart. (Special observations for caregivers may be found in Appendix B.)

When the book was first circulated among friends and family for their opinions on whether they found it was something someone else in a similar position might read, I had some interesting reactions. One was, why would I want to share something quite so revealing about myself? I questioned that myself when someone said, "I feel I know you both so much better!" My first reaction was: *Do I really want people to know me that well?*

After much inner questioning, I decided this was something I felt I should do, for the very reason I stated above: caregivers do not always let others know what they are experiencing. I believe most of us caregivers wonder: *If others really knew what I am like, would they approve, or even like me?* We hesitate to reveal those secret doubts even to our closest friends or family members.

It was interesting to me that after people had read my book, they became more open with sharing their feelings. My many years of working for Weight Watchers taught me about the effectiveness of sharing similar experiences, thus enabling others to relate to us more readily.

There are times when it is important to our mental and physical health to be able to share our fears, worries, and frustrations, as well as excitement, joy and love. We may have to learn how and when to do this and to whom. As we share, however, others will recognize common feelings and therefore feel more comfortable sharing their own inner thoughts.

*"A man who trusts men
will make fewer mistakes
than he who mistrusts them."*

May 28. The Spirit Has No Age

Have you ever voiced the thought that you don't feel older inside? It's only when you aren't able to do something at the same speed, or with the same ease you remember doing it formerly, that you feel old inside.

I saw a wonderful ballet that had been composed around the spirit of the choreographer's grandmother. He said age is energy and that spirit is also energy. He saw her not as slowing down, but filled with spiritual energy. The ballet very movingly and beautifully portrayed this spiritual energy.

Can you think of yourself as filled with spiritual energy after the physical energy leaves something to be desired in your mind? Consider the many things you have learned to deal with in your life. We celebrate the lives of those we love as well as those who passed in the night and met, but briefly. We can let their spirits go and don't feel constrained to justify their lives. There is joy that they passed through ours.

We learn to deal with losses and the fact that, many times, they come in bunches, leaving us no time to come to terms and regroup. I have become more assertive as I grow older. (Notice, I didn't say *old!*) Those who know me probably will laugh at my saying that, but there have been times when I would have done anything to avoid a confrontation. What changed? Maybe it was that spiritual energy that gave me courage to stand up for myself instead of backing off.

There are still those who tell me they envy my energy. I explain that what I still have is enthusiasm; the physical energy is no longer underneath. It is a matter of finding that spiritual energy to balance what I can and can no longer do physically and to be content with that knowledge. I do like the image of ourselves in our older years as being filled with spiritual energy to carry us forward.

Most of us have more than a nodding acquaintance with stress. That word actually has two meanings: one, to emphasize; the other, that well-known variety that sometimes turns our lives upside down. Our task is not to avoid stress, but to recognize and learn how to live with it. This is where our spiritual energy can come to our aid by influencing our attitude toward our lives, to help us find our stress level.

I have always felt energized when I was learning something new. This can bring back mental, physical, and spiritual energy to our lives. We still are free to choose our goals, and there must be goals—not just wishes—in our future. Let our lives be justified by our spiritual energy, not by our limitations.

*"I do not feel any age yet.
There is no age to the spirit."*

June 4. Nursing Home Phobia

From conversations with various friends, I have discovered that "Nursing Home Phobia" is very much alive and well in many of us at this stage of our lives. No one likes to contemplate such an end to a useful life.

When I required a short stay in such a facility, I did not need much more than simple TLC, and I was able to observe firsthand what life was like there. I watched and listened to the way both the very ill and the not-so-ill patients were cared for, and was very heartened by these observations. The shortage of nursing professionals is nation-wide, yet the available staff in the facility where I stayed managed to do their work with compassion and caring. I believe this is true in most well-regulated facilities.

Fearing the unknown is understandable. However, it appears to me that what we fear most is giving up control over our lives. Many of us have already dealt with some aspects of this loss as we grow older. However, it surprised me to learn that few of us visit such facilities until the need arrives, even avoiding visiting someone we know.

Since this type of care is one of the concerns of our age group, one would imagine that a nursing facility would be high on our priority list to inspect, including talking to residents there. It surprised me to read that the percentage of us who will need nursing home care is actually quite low. However, the present increase in diagnosis of Alzheimer's and other dementing diseases may alter those present statistics.

Because we are all taking better care of ourselves and living so much longer, if you have a concern that this is where you will end up someday, you need to educate yourself about nursing homes. Rather than trying to ignore your dread of having to go to a nursing home, why not see just what goes on? Don't rely on hearsay; see for yourself. This will enable you to face your fears, which is a big step to overcoming them. A fear, once faced, loses much of its power over you.

There are also ways *you* can make a difference in someone's life there. If you see things that need further attention in a facility you visit, get involved and perhaps help improve life for present as well as future residents. In so doing, you will relieve your own anxieties. Doing volunteer work has benefits of it's own.

If you have a known medical condition, learn as much as possible about your case, acquaint yourself with available facilities, and put that "Nursing Home Phobia" in the proper perspective. When you know as much about your own health as possible, you will feel more in control; that is the desired result.

"The past cannot be changed: the future is still in your power."

June 11. Time Priorities

How has your attitude toward time changed since you retired? When my husband and I moved to a retirement community, friends who hadn't made such a move usually asked, "What do you do with yourself?" Here's my answer: "There still isn't enough time for me to do all the things I want to do!" Even so, there is a difference these days. I am able to put off until tomorrow things I don't feel like doing. On the other hand, I can spend as much time on my hobbies as I am able—without feeling guilty!—for the first time in years.

Since I don't have unlimited energy, I am very choosy about what I do take on. In addition, I enjoy having times when I don't have to do anything! It's great to know if I don't pay the bills or go to the store today, I can get along fine until I want to do it. The pressure to be on a schedule every day no longer exists.

Many learn this long before they retire, but I was one of those busy people who was constantly on the move, and loved it. It took a serious illness to slow me down, and I fought that, too. I finally had to change a few things to adjust to my new energy level, and I find just as much fulfillment with a more relaxed attitude. Let me add, I'm a slow learner! When I have good days, I have a tendency to make up for what I didn't do on an off day, with predictable results. People who know me see me as a bundle of energy much of the time. What they don't see is when I'm flat, trying to recoup some of that "energy." When I remember my grandmother, I see her going full steam ahead or flat on her back. I admired her very much, and am amused that I seem to be cut from the same cloth.

There are still many activities I would like to explore, but I have eliminated many I used to say I wished I had learned to do. I realize that if I had really wanted to do them, I would have found the time. They were wishes, not goals. You need to be able to look forward to doing something new. It is better if you make new activities achievable—something you desire very much to do. That way, you are more likely to plan to do them.

To make time work for you, know what you truly want to do and start using your newfound time doing your "favorite things."

*"A thing is important
if anyone thinks it is important."*
—William James

June 18. Staying On Top

SOMEONE ONCE SAID THAT EVERYONE SHOULD move at least every ten years to clear out all those things we accumulate over the years! In like manner, we should take the time, every so often, to haul out and evaluate our attitudes about ourselves. We tend to carry along the same old ideas and opinions of our worth, character, intelligence, physical ability, willpower, and many other aspects of our lives. How many of these have any real basis any more?

Do you say, "I've always done it this way," or, "I'll never be able to change, it's just the way I am"? Do you resist change? Is there really a good reason why you can't change certain ways of dealing with your life? Of course, you would have to feel you would derive some benefit from this change. All of us tend to want to hold the old comfortable, familiar way of doing things.

Maybe now is a good time to bring these old familiar thoughts and attitudes into the open and take a good look at the messages you give yourself. Determine the ideas you recognize as needing to be adjusted for change. It can be very exciting to discover all the things you either thought you couldn't do, or have stopped doing, that turn out to be manageable. Each small success lets you know you do have the power, slowly perhaps, to make significant changes in your attitudes about your life and what you are capable of doing.

New ideas will also need to be evaluated from time to time. If they don't work out as you planned, were you too optimistic? Perhaps you set your goal too high and need to pull back to a more realistic one. These all have to be upgraded periodically after the changes get to be more of a habit. Remain receptive to new thoughts, attitudes, and actions. You can choose to continue to grow and expand your horizons.

Retain the ideas that work for you right now. Replace any discarded attitudes with new positive ones that will keep you moving forward instead of stagnating in the status quo.

Two quotes to inspire:

> *"The great end of life
> is not knowledge, but action."*
> —Aldous Huxley

> *"The greatest discovery of my generation
> is that human beings can alter their lives
> by altering their attitudes of mind."*
> —William James

June 25. Running in Place

EVERYWHERE WE LOOK THESE DAYS—magazines, newspapers and TV—experts (and others) are extolling the benefits of physical fitness for good health, weight control and well-being. Health clubs and gyms are doing very well, thank you!

Most of us were probably physically fit when we were growing up, only no one thought about it as such. We just walked everywhere! Our families also didn't have the many labor-saving devices we now enjoy. Those who grew up on farms or with a family business learned to work at an early age. Everyone was expected to contribute.

People appeared to be more physically fit formerly, but from what we hear about their diets in those days, perhaps they weren't as fit as we thought! People died a lot younger than they do now, many from heart disease and strokes. Today, we are more conscious about keeping track of fat and sugar and keeping our consumption of them within a safe range.

Today we have health clubs and gyms where there is state-of-the art equipment to help build and tone our muscles. There are also heated pools and exercise classes for those with arthritis, joint problems or injuries, who wish to improve their quality of life. Swimming itself is considered an ideal, all around exercise, except for developing good bones, which we need to do by bone stressing. This happens with weight bearing exercises, such as walking, running or climbing stairs. There are machines of all kinds to simulate jogging, walking and stair stepping. We need to find exercises that work to build up bone density to avoid osteoporosis as we grow older. I started wondering about doing all our exercises on machines. This seemed similar to running in place, which we used to do in gym classes.

Plain old walking is considered one of the safest and least expensive physical exercises (requiring no special equipment other than good shoes), and it is one of the most beneficial. It can also become an opportunity to appreciate nature and the passing scene. Join with a companion, and it turns into a social occasion. If you enjoy going alone, you can think about matters that need your attention, or you can daydream, becoming receptive to solutions. Safety is a prime consideration. If the neighborhood is not secure or the hour is late, malls are available. And they're air-conditioned! Health clubs and gyms fill this need, too, providing a safe place to exercise. Moreover, they offer a chance to meet others with similar goals.

Whatever course you follow, set your sights on a realistic goal, breaking it down into manageable segments to insure that you do not overestimate your abilities or endurance. Build your skills gradually and make sure you are going somewhere, not—literally and figuratively—running in place!

"Every journey starts with a single step."

July 2. Freedom

THERE ARE TWO KINDS OF FREEDOM: freedom *from*, and freedom *to*. Some of our most desirable freedoms are to be free *from* everything that keeps us from reaching the goals we have set for ourselves, to be free *from* using excuses or cop-outs, and—contrary to what seems to be fashionable these days—freedom *to* accept responsibility for our actions. We are never too old or infirm to set goals for ourselves. There are always challenges to be met, both lofty and the day-to-day kind. It is liberating to feel free to say, "I choose to," instead of "I ought to."

Freedom does not come easily. Remember how hard we had to work and sometimes, fight, to keep it in our country! It comes only through desire for change, our determination to be successful, and the discipline of following a plan that will help us get there. So often we say we lack "will power," but it is sometimes "won't power" that is stopping us in our tracks.

It's possible that what is lacking is a realistic plan. (I say this a lot!) If you dwell too long on what you consider your failure to follow through, you can easily become discouraged. An "attitude adjustment" from negative to positive is in order. It is important to break tasks into small, manageable steps.

If you aren't accustomed to walking any further than from the kitchen to the bedroom, it doesn't make sense to commit to walking a mile every day! We know drinking water is healthful, but if you now drink zilch, it is not realistic to aim for six a day right now. Start with a plan for five- or ten-minute walks at first, and to drink one extra glass of water daily. *Of course, I can do that!* There. You are successful already, once you are confident of your ability to succeed. If you are an old hand at starting things but poor at following through, you need quick success! You are free to do nothing, but if you are reading this, you probably won't be content to take that route forever. Somehow, you have to keep trying.

Review your priorities and redefine your goals, being realistic when it involves making changes. The ultimate freedom is to expand your horizons by being willing to risk making a commitment. You will become strong by believing in yourself.

> *"Habit is habit, and not to be flung out of the window by any man, but coaxed downstairs a step at a time."*
> —Mark Twain

July 9. How Good Is Good?

How many of us were admonished when we were growing up to be "good" and always to do "the right thing"? This led us to believe if we lived this way, everything would always come out right.

So we go by the book and somewhere along the line, our lives are not okay. Things *don't* go right! What is our first thought? "What did I do wrong?" Now we are obliged to take a good look at just who and what we really are and how we feel about our life at this point.

Perhaps you lived very confidently in your do-the-right-thing world, secure and feeling invulnerable. Then one day that confidence was shaken and you had to distill what really matters from your past actions. Now you have to build a new confidence in yourself, not merely because you are *good* and do the right thing. It must come from a deeper sense of your worth, belief that your basic principles are the right ones, plus knowledge gathered from your life experiences. You can then confront the challenges in positive ways, secure that your beliefs are right.

It is good if this happens early enough to enable you to reroute yourself. You often hear, "Who said life is fair?" Developing coping skills is a must, so you can proceed without wasting energy wondering what you did wrong. Looking back to a past experience and wondering, *What if I had . . . ?* is not a valid exercise in the present. For one thing, now that you are further down the road, you are likely to do things differently. Hindsight that's 20/20 plus further life experiences could suggest more productive solutions. Sometimes you have to put things in perspective, telling yourself you did the best you knew at the time, and let go.

Harboring guilt, bitterness, or anger can't undo the past, while letting go can bring peace of mind. I like the message in Matthew 6:34: "Take therefore no thought for the morrow: for the morrow shall take thought for the things of itself." You can live each moment, each day, and discover how peaceful that can be! You can put your thoughts of *being* good into *seeing* good in others. It is said that all problems can be solved with love, and that includes loving yourself as well.

"Shut out all of your past except that which will help you weather your tomorrows."

July 16. Confident, Not Complacent

BEING CONFIDENT IS VERY IMPORTANT to your self-esteem, but that is very different from being complacent. When you feel complacent, you are not opening your mind to new possibilities.

When you start thinking you have a handle on how to tackle challenges in your life, sometimes the old formulas don't appear to be working well. This can cause a lot of anxiety. You may even feel you have lost your ability to manage your situation. Having been in this position many times, I have discovered such times do pass; this is not the time to give up working to maintain your positive attitudes and the acceptance of what is. You must use all the skills you know to get yourself out of yourself. Ask the right questions, such as: "What can I do to improve this situation?" "How can I change my present attitude?" Stay away from "Why?" We seldom know the answer to that.

You can still practice the behaviors you know have worked for you in the past, even though they don't appear to be working now. You need to realize that sometimes none of your ideas will appear to work the way they are supposed to. This is the time to call upon your coping skills and decide to ride this out. The more you recognize yourself as capable, competent, strong, wise, loving and joyful, the more you will again believe it.

Searching out what needs to change and taking steps to effect this change is as important as recognizing what you have no power to change. Find the time and a quiet place to pray or get in touch with your *INNER WISDOM*. It will get you back on the road to being confident that you can make it through this temporary detour.

> *"Prayer is not a substitute for work.*
> *It is a desperate effort*
> *to work further and be effective*
> *beyond the range of one's power."*

July 23. Alone or Lonely?
"Loneliness expresses the pain of being alone, solitude—the joy!"
—Susan Smith Jones

How comfortable are you with your own company? Do you look forward to quiet times with yourself, or do you dread these moments alone? I always hated to have my husband go away on trips, but I also enjoyed doing just as I pleased for a little while, without having to take anyone else's wishes under consideration. I did not enjoy this over a long period, but for those few days, it was very comfortable.

Even when we live with someone, there is a need for moments of privacy. We need to allow each other this space. When you are handed some time to yourself, what do you like to do with it? Solitude can be a welcome respite where you can pursue a hobby, catch up on long-standing jobs, listen to beloved music, read or . . . just loaf! Solitude can be for remembering, gathering your thoughts, making plans, going through old pictures, and writing letters or journals. If you have problems occupying yourself, perhaps it would be helpful to question why.

Sometimes we feel alone because we think our problems are unique and no one else could understand. If we join a support group, we find that most people have similar sensations of being overwhelmed or discouraged and the same feelings of guilt, insecurity, sadness and anger, as well as joy.

When we are not happy with ourselves, we don't usually enjoy solitude because we tend to dwell on what we perceive are our shortcomings. We are not always anxious to face this. In a support group, we find people who have traveled our road and understand just how we feel. It doesn't have to be a labeled "support group"; it can be any time friends talk together. Perhaps we need to reach out to find a group in which we will feel secure.

If you have a strong religious faith, that can be a great springboard to finding opportunities with compatible groups of kindred spirits. Your group may be your own special friends.

Sometimes opening your eyes to the beauty and goodness around you can relieve loneliness. Become comfortable with and accept who and what you are. Know that you have done the best you could at any one time. Take advantage of moments alone for introspection as well as relaxation. Maybe you can bring joy to someone else who feels very alone. Reaching out to others is one of the best antidotes for loneliness and a way to turn loneliness—yours and theirs—into peaceful solitude.

"Nothing in life is to be feared; it is only to be understood."

July 30. Others See Us
*"Oh wad some power the giftie gie us
to see oursels as ithers see us!"*
—Robert Burns (*To a Louse*)

BURNS' LINE IS OFTEN PARAPHRASED in the statement that one sees himself as others see him. Charles Horton Cooley said, "Each to each a looking glass, reflects the other that doth pass," suggesting that the mirror works both ways. It seems more useful to me to phrase the concept this way: "Others see us as we see ourselves." With this statement, we refer to self-esteem.

It was my grandmother's custom to come to New York City once each year for a shopping and theater trip. Beginning when I was about 12, I would go into the city from New Jersey to spend some time with her. She was a large, imposing woman, and I became aware very early that when she "sailed" into a restaurant, the maître d' would always come running to serve her. She carried herself as though she were important, and that was the way she was treated. There was no doubt in my mind that she *was* important! However, this little observation stuck with me and evolved into my thinking that if one acted as if one were important, that would be the way she was treated!

I tried this out in various situations in my life, usually acting as though I were confident in a situation when I actually was scared to death. It worked!

During the years I worked for Weight Watchers, we encouraged our class members to act as though they were the weight they wished to be. They should not put off doing the things they had always wanted to do and be until they reached their goal weight, but to start to live *now*.

We are talking about accepting ourselves, going ahead with our lives, not waiting until every condition is perfect. This is about self-esteem. When you act as though you are a capable, confident person, your posture, the way you walk, smile and talk, manifests itself to others, either for better or worse. No one can give this to you; it has to come from within. Others can help foster this from the time you are born and nurture it all along the way with positive feedback. When you are grown, you have a choice to act in ways you would like to have others see you.

This means liking yourself—including your perceived shortcomings—patting yourself on the back for positive actions, walking proudly, smiling graciously and remembering your uniqueness. Look at yourself as you would like to be seen. Get on with your life rather than putting things off until you have reached a desired goal. Acting as though you have already arrived will do much more to get you there! Acting confident when you feel just the opposite helps you to feel that way! Others watching you will say it is so.

"You can preach a better sermon with your life than with your lips."

August 6. Know When to Say When

My wise mother used to say when something got to be too hard to do, she figured she wasn't supposed to do it! Most of us have run into situations where we wanted to do something very much, such as going on a particular trip or doing something else we had been looking forward to. Then we found we were tying ourselves in knots, trying to make it happen!

In such cases, I have learned to re-evaluate my goal to see if it is reasonable and realistic. The roadblocks seem to be there to send me a message that perhaps a change of plan is advisable. Usually another course of action opens up, one which clicks into place more easily. We then realize this is a much more realistic goal.

One Christmas I had been making plans to visit one of our children, but became aware that I was running into some challenges that indicated my visit would be more of a problem than a pleasure. They protested, but I found I had been perceptive in not going at that particular time. Their heating system went out of kilter and they had to live in a 58° house! Other complications arose as well. I believe I had ESP about that trip!

Maintaining your flexibility to shift to another plan is important as you grow older. It is hard to shift gears, but an alternate approach is often the wiser choice, perhaps one that hadn't even occurred to you previously. Sometimes it is a matter of accepting a situation and, thereby, finding it is something you can really be content with. That is wanting what you have. This doesn't mean you shouldn't have dreams and aspirations, for simply settling for the status quo can keep your life from going forward and growing. Still, when all kinds of obstacles keep popping up, it is sometimes more prudent to pull back, re-evaluate your goal and stop trying to make something happen that obviously isn't meant to be.

Conversely, attaining a desired goal bestows the reward of getting something you wanted. In both of these situations, there are no losers.

There is energy involved in these situations, as well. On the one hand, you recognized that perhaps your goal was unrealistic and were moved to accept a different one. Doing this without bitterness can foster growth by enabling you to know your limitations and to set your future goals with this knowledge.

Where a goal has been achieved, the satisfaction contributes to your self-esteem. Sometimes it happens without too much effort, but that is closer to serendipity. True achievement of a goal usually takes some planning on your part. Therefore your successes will teach you more about your abilities to carry out your plans.

We can find different activities, new skills (or time for old ones), new friends, perhaps new places! I find I'm not as anxious or stressed out

trying to do something that simply doesn't want to happen! I now tell myself to cool it long before it gets that far. It is obviously not meant to be.
When we find what we wanted doesn't occur, let's decide to want what does!

> *"Life is what happens*
> *when you've made other plans."*
> —Erma Bombeck

August 13. Obstacles

Do you ever run into an obstacle just when you think you are really getting going on a good, realistic goal? That probably happens more often than not! We have been advised to find a way around, over, under or through such an obstacle when it lies in our path.

There is a good saying I have mentioned before: "If there is no solution, there is no problem." In other words, don't go crazy trying to find a solution when it is more a matter of acceptance. Many of us waste a lot of good time on that one!

When I was about three years old, my mother was taking me upstairs for my nap. Outside, a severe summer thunderstorm was raging. We had an enclosed stairwell, with a blank, outside wall at the top. Suddenly a bolt of lightening hit a large pine tree directly outside, and for an instant, that wall became transparent. My mother and I *saw* the lightening hit that tree! If Mother hadn't verified my memory of that event, I would think I had imagined it.

I don't recall any discussions of the phenomenon, but I'm sure some took place in the family. With the present advances in the studies of atoms and molecules, and even smaller particles in our world, I have come to believe that a powerful charge of electricity can very well alter the composition of matter temporarily, and possibly, permanently.

That was certainly an unusual experience, but how can we relate it to solving the presence of solid walls in the path of our goals? Simply, it is to look upon obstacles as something that can possibly be altered. The hindrance may not be as solid as we, at first, perceive it to be. There may be some innovative way, not considered previously, to approach the obstacle and turn it into an opportunity. On the other hand, we may have to work at accepting that wall and turn on to another path.

Consider this concept and know that you don't have to figure it out by yourself. Look to your Higher Power for guidance and ask: "Why is it opportunities always look bigger going than coming?"

"Obstacles are those frightful things you see when you take your eyes off your goal."

August 20. Who Are You?

To YOU AND YOUR WORLD, the most important living person is *you*. You are a body with a mind.

Let us think about this mind of ours. It is divided into two parts: a conscious and an unconscious, and it has two attitudes: positive and negative. Our subconscious mind works under a universal law that says, "What the mind can conceive and believe, the mind can achieve." We become what we think about. How does this happen?

Compare the human mind to a fertile field. It contains good soil and it doesn't care what is planted in it; anything will grow, weeds or grains. The field will return what we plant. The mind works in much the same way. It doesn't care what information we feed it, whether it is success or failure. The mind, too, will return what we plant.

What are you planting in your mind these days? Do you want to harvest happiness? Start by thinking happy thoughts. Tell yourself you *are* happy and act as though you *are* happy. Do you want to reap self-confidence? Tell yourself, "I am a poised, self-confident person!" Do you want to raise a crop of successes? Decide on a realistic, *specific* goal and tell yourself you are successful; then *act* as though you are already there.

When you feel self-doubts creeping back, replace those doubts with confidence in your success. If you feel yourself succumbing to an "I can't!" attitude, remember that "I can't" is not a fact; it means, "I won't," and it is an idea you or someone else has sold you. It will lose its hold over you if you cease to believe it. Replace it with the positive "I can!"

A little practice in acting like a happy, confident person will eventually become the real thing. Think *positive*, think *thin*, think *success*!

> *"Only one person in the world
> can defeat you,
> that is* yourself.*"*

August 27. Forgiveness

MOST OF US HAVE, AT SOME TIME IN OUR LIVES, been faced with whether we could deal with forgiving someone who "done us wrong." There may have been a big hurt, or the situation may not have been serious at all. In any case, if you were brought up to forgive your enemies, you found yourself uncomfortable with your inability to do it upon this occasion.

For the big hurts, it will take time to work through your fragmented emotional responses. Perhaps you are able to arrive at the point where you can forgive your enemy, but you certainly don't want ever to have anything to do with that person again. You feel as though you have forgiven, but you find that anger, maybe even revenge, still intrudes on your thoughts from time to time. This is not true forgiveness.

In a workshop I attended, the discussion was about resolving unfinished business with others, even when that person was out of touch or deceased. We were instructed to get into a very relaxed state and have an imaginary conversation with the subject of our anguish. Once we are able to verbalize mentally and share our feelings about the unfinished business, it was a great surprise to discover we could actually have a silent dialogue and almost hear and feel the other person's responses.

Try it. You'll find it quite amazing that once you organize your thoughts on the matter, you will feel the release you never thought you would experience because the other party is no longer available. If the other person *is* accessible, sometimes this exercise will help you feel the situation is on its way to being resolved.

Deep down, we realize most people do not intentionally hurt others, yet when they do, we quickly lose sight of any good we used to see in them. It is important to remember we also have the power to *give* mercy and forgiveness. The other person may not feel the need for our forgiveness, but we need to give it, for our own peace of mind.

When we can't do it by ourselves, we must "Let go and let God."

*"It isn't the load that weighs us down,
it's the way we carry it."*

September 3. Hypochondria

ONE OF OUR CHILDREN TOLD ME he thought I was much too concerned about my health problems and that I talked about them too much. Strangely, this did not offend me; in fact, I agreed with him. Living in a retirement community with the population pretty limited to one age group, it is very easy to succumb to this pastime. In a more varied community, there would be more opportunities to speak—along with Lewis Carroll's Walrus—"of many things, Of shoes—and ships—and sealing wax—Of cabbages—and kings . . ."

I remember a conversation with my bridge club, when we were probably in our forties, where we all declared we would *never* fall into the habit of talking about our ailments! Most of us were experiencing our aging parents' problems with what we called "organ recitals!" My own mother fell into that trap, too, and didn't recognize she was doing the very thing she had deplored. It seems the wheel rolled around to me as well!

Many of us become overly concerned with the effects of aging on our bodies, with the attendant difficulties adjusting to these effects. This can lead to our seeking information or solace from our friends and family. Occasionally, we all need someone with whom we feel comfortable discussing such things.

It helps to notice what we talk about on a day-to-day basis with friends and family. If the state of our health is the primary topic, it is time to plan our conversations to include more varied subjects. This is not an easy task if we have become preoccupied with ourselves a good bit of the time.

Recognizing a problem is the first step to solving it, so the first step is to listen to others and ourselves. I find that most of the "organ recitals" are done with good humor, with a more "What's next?" connotation than true complaint.

All of this being true, it behooves us to become conscious of our conversations. "A bore is someone who insists on talking when you want them to listen." Those of us who enjoy conversing can, no doubt, recall times when a good discussion was in progress and we found ourselves just waiting for the speaker to take a breath so we could jump in with our contribution! If we are doing this, we are not really listening to the speaker, but thinking more about what we want to say. Of course we may have reached the point in our lives when we forget what we want to say if we don't get to say it the second the thought occurs!

Maintaining a sense of humor about yourself is so important. This is the time to evaluate your listening as well as communication skills. Become less concerned with yourself and more concerned with others, at the same time remaining interested in what's going on in the world.

It is possible to change an irritating habit once we become aware of it. After all, we don't want to bore others! It will take a lot of concentration to stay away from our favorite subject: ourselves. But this is a good way to expand our interests. Maybe if we don't think about ourselves as much, we will actually feel a lot better!

> *"Be the best that you can be, because that's all you have!"*

September 10. Computer Gap

MANY OF US WATCH WITH WONDER the new language of the computer generation. Perhaps we are curious and intrigued, wishing we could understand some of the wonders these new machines can accomplish in the blink of an eye! Our grandchildren and even great grandchildren pick up these skills at such an early age, surely we could manage it! All we need is an interest in learning about computers.

A computer is a pretty expensive toy if you don't have a use for it, but if you write or do bookkeeping, you will find it can make your tasks much simpler. Letter writing and keeping track of your checkbooks, accounts and investments are good reasons to look into this new skill. You'll learn that it is just a machine that you can tell to carry out a command and it will do it.

Usually, as novices, we are scared of doing something terrible, since we have heard stories of awful frustrations from the most seasoned operators. Many of us start learning to use a computer to be able to speak the language of our children and grandchildren. The children will often write us on e-mail when they wouldn't bother to write and mail a letter. This is where the computer becomes a bridge between the generations.

Probably the principal use for a computer will be

word processing, a function similar to a typewriter, except that the former does extraordinary things to help in editing and checking spelling and grammar. The spreadsheet function helps most users keep accounts and financial affairs. It is not as difficult to use these machines as we imagine before we begin.

Learning to operate a computer has a surprising benefit. It offers something to do with your spare time after retirement. It is a new challenge and a lot of fun. It becomes very addictive, and once you learn your way around the Internet, the world opens up to all kinds of information on any subject you can think of. There are chat rooms where you can type conversations with people sharing your interests. You can also get your news and weather, moment to moment, if you like; do research on any subject effortlessly; explore a myriad other marvels. Here is a skill that can keep you as occupied as you wish to be. You can also shop at your favorite stores by name . . . but, perhaps, we'd better keep a check on that!

Computer operators I know have discovered surprising benefits. Some friends told me they had become discouraged by the options left to them in retirement, wondering what to do with their spare time. They found learning to operate a computer a new challenge they were well able to master, and it filled their time once they discovered all the things it could do for them. For them, there is no longer a problem with having too much spare time.

Using a computer is a skill that can keep us as busy as we want to be, and out of mischief. It can be used as a tool to help others, and it reassures us that we can still learn new tricks. Explore this new dimension and discover the bridge to the future!

"Nobody can think straight who does not work. Idleness warps the mind. Thinking without constructive action becomes a disease."
—Henry Ford

September 17. Posture

ARE YOU AWARE OF THE MANY ADVANTAGES of good posture? My mother used to poke me in the middle of my back all the time and tell me to "stand up straight!" I never realized all the extra good things that come with good posture until I read an article about it in a magazine.

For whatever reason you slump, it can cause a lifetime of minor ailments: lower back and shoulder spasms, decreased lung capacity, and other chronic pains. Most of these can be avoided or helped if you remember when standing, sitting or walking, to get in the habit of relaxing your shoulders, rotating them up and back. Feel like a puppet on a string that is fastened to the middle of your chest, pulling up behind your ears. Look straight ahead instead of at your feet. If you are fearful of falling, you needn't take chances, but you can look ahead for obstacles. This helps avoid "dowager's hump," that bump at the base of the neck. Hold your head high and see how much better it feels to stand as straight as you are able.

Osteoporosis may mean not being able to straighten completely any more, but you can become more conscious of your posture. Improving it may take practice. Slumping makes anyone look and feel more tired or discouraged. Standing or sitting tall will make you look and feel better in spite of yourself. Regard yourself not as a finished product, but as a work in progress.

*"We are never too old
to improve our lives!"*

September 24. Take Advantage

In FACING THE NEGATIVES OF GROWING OLDER, have you discovered some of the definite advantages? Quite a few years ago I recognized that I was no longer obliged to do many of the activities I had been unable, in the past, to say no to. Now I can say no and don't feel I have to explain or feel guilty about it.

There's no doubt that we no longer have the limitless energy we were accustomed to, so now we are at liberty to make choices as to what we will do and what we will leave undone. I have never been what one would call a meticulous housekeeper. I did enough to keep things respectable and sanitary, but it wasn't my main concern.

My mother used to say if we took care of BBD (beds made, bathrooms clean, dishes done) we could get by. For most of my adult life I had a hard time going out early without taking care of those tasks. There were times when I had to leave them undone, which left me feeling faintly guilty. I got over it.

I am in favor of making lists of things to be done, with degree of importance and time required. When we take on something essential, we should feel free to leave the beds or the dishes . . . or turn off the phone. I was never able to do that last; I always thought the call might be important. If it were, of course, the caller would try again or find someone else to do it. We can relax and follow our activity priorities before we take on the "have to" tasks. They will be there later.

Learn to avoid over-committing yourself. You can now take charge of what you choose to do with your time. It's possible you will have to practice saying, "I choose to," or, "I choose not to," instead of "I can't." You can now convince yourself that it is fine to take care of what you feel is important in your life, in terms of both people and activities. By using the talents and interests you have, conforming to the energy available, you will find you can be happy even if you aren't traveling in the fast lane, but leisurely, at the back of the pack!

"The race is not always to the swift, but to those who keep running."

October 1. Changing Others

Can you recall wishing you could get someone else to change? Did you try? How successful were you?

I have learned that in order to get someone else to change, we have to first change ourselves! This is the starting point: Instead of praying or entreating the other person to change, whom do we have the power to change? Ourselves, of course, and it begins with a change in *our* attitude.

Examine how you feel about this other person you wish to change. Is he or she important to you? Where your faith comes into play is by praying to change the way you see the other person. Pray to accept this person you love *as is*, and trust they will be directed to find their own way to wisdom, prosperity, patience, and tolerance, relying on the good you know is in them. Often, when you remove the pressure, people are more likely to change those very characteristics themselves.

If you have raised children, you recognized very early that your little baby was born with a mind of his or her own. You tried to guide and teach your children the things you felt they needed to know to cope with life, you hoped, by your example. From your own experience, you remember you had to make your own mistakes, and usually, they weren't fatal. Your children or good friends have to be allowed to do the same, because you believe in the good in them.

It is hard to give them that freedom and hold your tongue when you see them making unwise choices even when they are mature, but it is a different story if they seek your advice. When they question their ability to handle certain situations, your prior experiences can help them recognize options. These are offered not as a parent or authority, but as equals. This avoids preaching and approaches them on an adult level.

I recall a therapist asking me if I didn't approve of our children's final decision, could I still accept it and let them go. That was a difficult question, but I believe I'm getting the hang of it.

Let us exhort ourselves to look for the good in others and accept them as they are. Perhaps this will be a giant step toward the changes we'd like to see. We need to express our opinion if the behavior is wrong, unhealthy or illegal, but let's not beat the subject to death. Changing our own attitudes by not being judgmental is difficult, since often life is not fair. Sometimes, nothing works, and we have to accept that as well.

"Prayer is not overcoming God's reluctance; it is laying hold on His willingness."

October 8. Avoiding Accidents

Dr. C Everett Koop, former U.S. Surgeon General, did a television series on helping seniors avoid accidents. The one that impressed me most was when he explained how important it is to get up from a chair correctly. He demonstrated that the worst thing we can do is to try to stand up from a seated position with our knees angled out. Using a model of the hip and thigh bones, he pointed out that the weakest part of that combination is the part between the top of the thigh bone and the hip ball. When we angle our knees out, we are putting the weakest part under great twist and stress. The times this is done are when a lot of hip fractures occur. If we have osteoporosis, it is often a point of conjecture whether the bone broke first and we then fell, or the other way around.

Dr. Koop's suggestion was to be sure we move ourselves to the front edge of whatever we are seated upon, plant our two feet parallel, our knees straight ahead, then push ourselves up, using our arms if necessary. An exercise useful in developing more strength in our thigh muscles is called a "modified squat."

Grasp the back of a chair (in front of you) and squat as though you were going to sit. It is not necessary to move very far in this, just enough so you can feel the pull of your thigh muscles. Start with a few repetitions and increase when you feel able to add a few more.

Walking will build leg muscles as well, and for those with knee and foot problems, walking in water will help, too. I can't repeat often enough that before trying any new exercise routine, you need to get your doctor's permission and advice.

Dr. Koop suggested another way to avoid falls is to notice the hazards around your home. Cupboard doors are a hazard, as well as small throw rugs that have lost their rubber backing and curl up or move. When I start to trip over the edges of throw rugs, they really become *throw* rugs!

There is a big incentive to keep your floors safe. Watch for things you might trip over, such as electric cords, or items left on the floor that you can slip on. Avoid lifting heavy loads, since the old shoulders are more fragile than they used to be. Outdoors, look for slippery stones and raised or sunken places on the walks. Check your stove and electrical appliances to be sure they are turned off or unplugged. These cautions are good for any age. When we had young children, we child-proofed our homes by removing hazardous chemicals and medications. Now we accident-proof our homes for ourselves. We don't have to become helpless, just prudent and observant.

"There is only a slight difference between keeping your chin up and sticking your neck out, but the difference is worth knowing!"

October 15. Letting Go

LETTING GO! THAT FOLLOWS right after acceptance and can apply to so many aspects of our lives.

Perhaps the biggest hurdle is letting go of control of your life. But think about it. How much control do you really have anyway? When you can't seem to let go of something, take a look at what you are trying to control. None of us can control other people, and most of the time, we have little control over various events in our own lives. Getting older, for instance. Everyone does it and, considering the alternative, the choice isn't so bad. It is necessary to let go of yesterday. This involves thinking creatively of some new ways to use what we have left, rather than mourning what we used to be.

Many of us, when we retire, move to a smaller residence. There is a tendency to bring too many things along with us when we have to downscale. I believe this is due to our wanting to keep as much as possible of our past life with us. That is very important; however, as we settle into our new home, we are better able to separate the really special possessions and let go of the rest. And so we are able to let go of items from the past.

Letting go of well-loved clothes that no longer fit is not as easy as it sounds. Hope springs eternal, and we always hope we'll be able to wear a particular outfit again. Having battled this particular state of mind—I hate to think of how many times!—I finally learned that when I did lose some weight, I generally wanted something new anyway.

Letting go of unrealistic goals may actually motivate us. If you move to a new locality, there is always the goal of making new friends. Getting into new activities is a great way to meet new people. Avoid overdoing it, however. When I went off to college, my mom warned me not to make friends too fast, and that's good advice at any age. You might find new friends don't wear well, or the activities you jumped into might not suit your interests, after all. Establish your own priorities and guard against being over-involved. I find I'm delighted when I have days with nothing scheduled. Could it be there is nothing wrong with slowing down some?

One of the hardest tasks is letting go of the image of a loved one who is failing. We hate to give up on having to have all the answers. Let go and get help if you need it. Every step down means facing letting go every time circumstances change.

You can apply this to many aspects of your life. There has to be a letting go of old behaviors and old ideas. However, today can be just as wonderful even if it is different. It is called living in the *now*. If you manage to do that, it will be much easier to accept future challenges.

> "Do the very best you can
> and leave the outcome to God."

October 22. Making Minutes Count

ARE WE STILL CAUGHT UP IN THE OLD ADAGE of making every minute count? My husband had the very handy talent of being able to break down into words and communicate the motions required to go through a task successfully. I tried to show our boys how to tie their shoes, but Tony could talk them through the motions, and they learned much more quickly. People who do this for a living are called "time-motion specialists" and are well paid and in demand. Companies are very interested in saving precious time in their business affairs.

When we retire, we have to face what we are going to do with all the minutes we have saved all our lives. We know many retirees who are very happily occupied doing things they perhaps didn't have time for previously. If we wonder why we didn't get around to doing it before, one answer might be that we are now more focused. It is equally important to lose our guilt over wasting time when we feel like it.

Another old adage is: "If you want to get a job done, ask a busy person to do it." It's not just finding the time, but being able to concentrate our energy or attention on what we want to accomplish. Busy people are generally more organized. It appears to help if we don't have to be concerned about our time. I, for one, hate to feel rushed. If we don't pressure ourselves, we probably do a better job and have more fun doing it.

We also notice there is sometimes a difference in the way men and women regard time. According to an article about this subject, "Don't Make Every Minute Count," by Michael Korda, men are better at rationalizing when they secretly feel they are wasting time; women, on the other hand, are usually more uncomfortable about the whole idea. Somewhere this was drummed into us while we were maturing. Many women have developed skills along the way by volunteering, doing church work, acquiring social skills, developing natural talents, and in the present day, many women—either because they must or it is their choice—have careers of their own.

Some people become so engrossed in their work that they have not developed outside interests, subsequently finding themselves floundering with newly found time on their hands when they retire. For some of us, there isn't enough time to do everything we want to; others may wonder how they will occupy themselves in these golden years they thought they were looking forward to.

You may get restless in your search, but help is within reach. Volunteering is rewarding both to the do-er and the do-ee. Without the pressure to save those precious minutes, there are many fields in which you we can make a difference. Think about things you have wanted to learn more about. How about taking a course or two? You will be surprised to find you rarely have to worry about whether you can keep up. It is rewarding to find how your years of experience will help you, by having better work habits and knowing you are there because you want to learn. If the course you choose doesn't work out as you had hoped, there's no reason you can't switch to something more to your liking. You have a solid savings account of minutes saved and earned. If you know where you want to go, you will find yourself very motivated. Use all those minutes saved and become a big spender from your time account!

> *"Time is only worth saving*
> *if you know what to do*
> *with the time you save."*
> —Michael Korda

October 29. Nature's Way

A SEMINAR LEADER STARTED WITH THIS STATEMENT: "In Nature there are no rewards and no punishments, only consequences." When I thought this over, it essentially said to me that Nature makes no judgments. I suppose we can include ourselves under the heading of Nature; therefore, if we do "A," we can expect "A" consequences. We can be fairly accurate at predicting consequences under the most familiar circumstances in our daily lives.

As I grow older (and wiser, I hope!) I find I am less inclined to be judgmental. I have learned that, since I have no way of being in another person's head, there is no way I can understand the many things that influenced that individual in a particular behavior. In turn, I hope others will afford me the same leeway.

As I have written before, we sometimes find ourselves trying to make another person change his or her behavior. We hear over and over the only person we have the ability to change is ourselves. However, we are also instructed that by changing our own attitude and the way we tend to judge this person, we are more likely to achieve the change we had hoped for.

When someone tries to get you to change a behavior, what is likely to be your first reaction?

Usually, you will get defensive, feel guilt or, possibly, shame. When you make a decision to accept other people the way they are, you can remove a lot of the reasons for defensive or destructive behaviors. Over time, this person may come to feel safe from attack, and more able to make his/her own changes.

On the other hand, you may feel you are not able to accept another's behavior as it is now. This is a decision one must make prayerfully. Not every interpersonal relationship has a black or white solution, and you must decide what shades of gray you can accept.

In this situation, it is good if there is acceptance of the circumstances on both sides, otherwise at least one side will continue to carry the frustration, anger or guilt. The word "co-dependent" is much used these days, and it is appropriate to realize that our reactions to unacceptable behaviors are often feeding those very behaviors. We become what are now called "enablers."

No rewards, no punishments, only consequences.

Each of us must establish the parameters of the black, white and gray we will accept. Then we may learn to love, forgive and accept each other as the unique beings we are. That is when we can live up to the limitless potential present in all of us.

"A big man is not one who makes no mistakes, but one who is bigger than any mistake he makes."

November 5. Against the Tide

The first time I swam in the ocean, I was instructed that if I ever found myself caught in an outgoing (rip) tide, I should not attempt to swim against it to shore, but parallel to the shore, across the current. The reasoning behind this advice was that these currents are not usually very wide, and it is easier to swim across them than to battle against them while being swept out. This way, the swimmer has a chance to get out of the tidal effect without tiring himself.

Sometimes in your life, you may find yourself battling the current and getting nowhere. You spend a lot of energy trying to overcome that current, when the best policy might be to see if there is a way to get across it. You might even enjoy the ride. Something that looked so overpowering to you when you were fighting it, might prove to be manageable when you either go across it or along with it.

If you are a water lover as I am, you have probably watched the waves, perhaps when you were troubled. There is something very calming, watching the regular flowing in and out of the waves when they meet the shore. You look out at the sea and observe the very large waves as they come rolling in with a great splash and roar, but as they wash up on the beach, they all end up a wash of water over the sand. When they run out again, there are none of those fearful breaking crests.

I can see how we could look at the events of our lives in this light. There may appear to be much sound and fury and overwhelming breakers that frighten us, and we feel so powerless. Perhaps it is necessary to watch and wait to examine that wave when it closes in on the shore, then becomes bubbles and ripples running out to sea so quietly.

When we learn about total relaxation, one of the techniques is concentrating on our breathing. We are taught to imagine waves rolling in and out, matching our breathing to this picture. We find our breathing slowing, our muscles relaxing and tension lessening.

Think about the difference between swimming against the tide and going with it. You may often wear yourself out and find you are more at sea than you thought. Don't panic! Swim across or with the current and get to where you want to be.

*"Peace is not the absence of conflict,
but the ability to cope with it."*

November 12. Self-Esteem

How do you define what makes you like or dislike who you are?

Several recent studies show how important to our self-esteem is the way our families related to us while we were growing up. Apparently this is something else to dump on Mom, but it is also true that Father has an impact on his children's feelings of self-worth. A man with exceptionally high standards can inspire his children to excel or give them the idea that it will be impossible to live up to his expectations. Reactions to this kind of pressure can vary from one child to another in the same family. It was interesting to me to observe how our three boys differed so much from each other. The birth order can have a big influence, and so can each child's unique personality, which is there from birth.

As children mature, some will give up trying to meet our expectations and some will go in the opposite direction. How fathers regard and treat their adolescent daughters also can have an enormous impact on their self-esteem and their future relationships with the men in their lives.

The interaction between mothers and their babies, from very early stages, is documented as being influential in the development of a child's perception of self. *The Perfect Woman*, by Dowling, cites studies taken from videotapes, as well as observations, that show the ways mothers tune in to their babies' feelings and reactions. With subsequent follow-ups, it has been found that instinctive mirroring or approval encourages the healthy development of a good self-image. When the child's actions are either misread or ignored, it can result in the child's feeling powerless or unworthy. I suspect that most of our parents, and we, fall somewhere in the middle of the ideal.

We can get away with blaming all our shortcomings and disappointments on our parents for only a short while. Once we are grown, we are obliged to accept responsibility for our own actions, successes and failures. It is up to us to decide what kind of a person we want to be, then go ahead and find our own esteem. We must learn to treat ourselves gently, especially if that was not the way we were treated at home.

When we consider all the things that can be done wrong in parenting, it's a wonder anyone turns out well. Now it is essential to recognize how you judge your own self-worth. Do you feel defined mainly by your accomplishments or lack of them? Or by your occupation? Or do you admire your uniqueness? On that fact alone, you can know humility and pride. It's important to love and accept the uniqueness that is yours. To be able to see that uniqueness in others is true self-esteem.

"If you had it to do over, would you fall in love with yourself again?"

November 19. Stress

When most of us think of stress, we associate it with unpleasant situations. Dr. Hans Selye gave stress its name as recently as forty years ago, describing it as the way our bodies react to all the ups and downs of our daily lives. It is the body's reaction to any demand placed upon it, pleasant or otherwise—the dentist's chair or a lover's kiss.

Some years ago I experienced what was diagnosed as a "stress burnout," which resulted in my feeling completely overcome with what was going on in my life at the time. I had thought I was managing my husband's diagnosed dementia quite adequately, but I soon learned that our bodies can't be fooled and that I was going to have to learn to manage my stress much more realistically. My method was to read everything I could get my hands on about the causes and effects of stress, and what actions to pursue to improve the way I handled my life.

In my reading, I found it was most important to learn to recognize my own responses to stress, since no two people respond the same way. It involves planning to structure one's life in the future to be able to live with that new understanding. Medication and/or counseling may be indicated, but there are other avenues we can explore to help rearrange our stress reactions.

I studied deep muscle relaxation from an excellent book, *The Doctor's Guide to Instant Stress relief*, by Nathan and Staata. The text helped me recognize my own responses, as well as teaching me how to relax different parts of my body when needed.

Meditation, prayer and physical exercise are additional means to help you stay calmer. When possible, taking a short walk will dispel a lot of the stress you are building. The advantage of these actions is that they occupy your mind and body with something else to think about, forcing the stressful thoughts temporarily from your conscious mind.

A recipe for managing stress is to first find your own stress level, decide if you are a turtle or a hare, and not be bashful about living your life accordingly. It has been difficult for me to adjust to not being a "hare" right now; I am more in the "turtle" category. Sometimes you may feel you can't take the time for yourself because of your responsibilities, but as I discovered, I'm not much help to anyone if I become overwhelmed myself!

There are many excellent books on this subject in bookstores and in libraries. They explain the chemistry and physical effects of stress on the body. By learning to become conscious of your own stress patterns, you can plan ahead to *make* the necessary time for managing your situation by reducing tension.

As with many problems, a positive attitude can make a great difference. Believing in yourself and recognizing that there are things you can do will help you take that first giant step toward become more in control and finding peace and calm where there was chaos with your Life Stressors.

"Know enough to know enough not to!"

November 26. Right Questions/Right Answers

WHEN YOU ARE ATTEMPTING TO MAKE SENSE out of what is going on in your life, are you aware that asking the right questions helps you get right answers? For instance, have you ever caught yourself asking: "Why? Why me? Why do I have to deal with this?"

Along with the why, perhaps you find yourself asking, "What did I do wrong?" Many of us feel guilty when things do go wrong, and that could well be your initial reaction. Actually, "what" is not a bad start for a good question; you just have to rephrase it. Sometimes you have to recognize how your previous choices played a big part in what is happening now. This is the first step toward accepting responsibility for your actions. The next "whats" could be, "What can I do differently?" "What changes can I make?" "What baggage am I carrying still?" "What can't be changed?"

We progress to the next good questions: "How can I handle this differently?" "How can I change?" These are good questions that can point us to good, positive solutions. Here is another: "When is it time to let go and ask for help?" This can be one of the most difficult questions we will have to answer.

Many times, right answers involve a change of attitude. If you don't keep a good rein on your reflections, you can find yourself in a negative, despairing frame of mind too easily. It is a good idea to have a set of positive affirmations to repeat to yourself when you sense you are slipping into that depression. If you consider them honestly, you probably do feel confident and capable much of the time.

You can make and have made wise decisions. You have been strong enough to make it through lots of obstacles in your life. You love and are loved, and there is still much joy all around you. You know there is order in the universe. You can't always see the direction that order is leading you, but you must have discovered things generally work out for good.

One of our sons had a close brush with death from toxic shock several years ago. He said that experience altered the way he viewed a lot of things. Among them, his advice was, "Don't sweat the small stuff, Mom." His words hit home since I feel I over-reacted to the "small stuff" much of the time when we were bringing up our boys. It was probably high time I took his advice.

In trying to find the right questions, examine the kinds of questions you usually ask yourself. Asking the right ones will carry you much further toward conquering your fears as well as viewing the ultimate solutions to your problems in a more positive fashion. *Believe* that you can find those right answers.

> *"The only ideas that will work for you are the ones you put to work."*

December 3. Packaging

WHEN DECEMBER ROLLS AROUND, it is sometimes hard for me to believe. They say, "Time flies when you are having fun," but the time seems to go faster these days! Christmas catalogues I used to receive shortly after Halloween now start coming at the end of summer. Even longer ago, I never did much serious shopping before Thanksgiving.

It's such a happy season! We think of the friends we don't usually hear from the rest of the year, and we enjoy putting much thought into just the right greeting or gift for those we love. When the shopping is finished, we take extra pains to wrap the gifts to look beautiful for this joyous season. Some gifts come already packaged in boxes we would recognize as special, even if the gift had not been wrapped, such as from a recognized luxury shop. We know we are in for something special when we see one of these! When it is also wrapped in attractive paper and trimmed beautifully, we eagerly anticipate the contents. The packaging certainly affects how we view the gift initially, even if later we find it contains a golden box. Perhaps we don't want to admit this, but it is very human.

How do you package yourself? Can you say, truthfully, "What you see is what you get"? When you meet someone new, are you a creatively wrapped package that shows you care a lot about what you present? I'm sure you hope you are not only what you look like, but are also like that beautiful golden box that contains something precious and unique. How do you show the world what you really are? You have to project the fact that you accept who and what you are, as you are. You must love and accept yourself, thus helping others to accept you the same way.

It's up to you to package yourself as attractively as possible to show you think enough of yourself to offer others the anticipation of opening this package, to discover the special person you are. The opposite tack is when it is obvious that you are not taking pains to make the most of your good points, refusing to present the most attractive wrapping possible.

People eventually will see past a paper bag, but they will be more likely to explore a special and unique package if that is what you project.

May our shopping and wrapping remind us of the one gift we all have to give—ourselves—and may our golden box show through all the beautiful wrappings. (Subject suggested by Al Super.)

> *"Good Nature will always supply*
> *the absence of beauty;*
> *but beauty cannot supply*
> *the absence of good nature."*

December 10. Tackle Christmas Early

THIS IS NOT ABOUT DOING YOUR SHOPPING EARLY, but being aware of the many food temptations you will face over the holidays. You may not have to watch your diet, but many times, all the rich and unaccustomed foods can be a problem. I always feel the world becomes a giant food pusher this time of year. It is imperative to tackle Christmas early!

For me, this means planning ahead not only for how I will deal with holiday temptations, but also managing my time. It helps me to consider the many pleasant aspects of the season that are not connected with food. Even those of us who do not normally have eating problems can find seasonal goodies contributing to the belt's being a little tight as well as the consequences of more rich foods than we are accustomed to. The media do a good job of selling the nostalgia that plays on past memories, usually heavily associated with smells and sights of holiday foods. We remember childhood Christmas or Hanukkah with Mother and Grandmother working hard to turn out the wonderful-smelling foods we will forever associate with this time of year.

We can use the nostalgia to enhance our celebrations by reflecting what means most to us instead of using it as an invitation to indulge in foods with which we would not normally be concerned. Take time to reflect during these holidays. For me, exchanging greetings with family and old friends I no longer see as often is one of the things I treasure most.

There is something about the season that builds tension, simply as the pace of our lives quicken. When I find this happening, I know it is time to take a deep breath and take "time out." This need not be a long time; 15-30 minutes to relax, off by myself, can work miracles to reduce tension. Perhaps it is your delight to indulge in a long, soaking bath, or to listen to well-loved, soothing music. You know what relaxes you.

Plan to continue your ordinary physical activities throughout the holidays. Even if you feel too fatigued to do it, take a short walk, swim or attend your usual exercise class. This can recharge your batteries and will leave you revitalized.

Here is my list of First Aid and Preventive Medicine for the Holidays:

>Drink lots of water.
>Continue to eat a balanced diet.
>Exercise regularly, if possible.
>Take time for yourself.
>Do something for someone less fortunate.
>Telephone an old friend.
>Get plenty of rest.
>SOCIALIZE!

At the party:
>Never arrive hungry.
>Take what you have decided to eat and move away from the food table.

REMEMBER THE REASON FOR THE SEASON.

December 17. Share Your Memories

WHAT ARE YOUR EARLIEST MEMORIES? What kind of a child were you? It has been theorized that our earliest memories give some clue to the kind of person we would become. Those who remember *feelings* of very early events are more likely to be right brain people. These folks are usually very creative and responsive to their own and others' feelings. Those whose early memories are more about people are more likely to be skilled in the practical sciences (left-brained).

My earliest memory is of standing in my crib, near a window overlooking my grandmother's garden. I was very conscious of the beauty of the sunlight on the green grass and the flowers. I can still see that picture in my mind. Mother told me I had to have been about two, since they took me out of my crib about that time. No one could have told me this, so it must be a valid memory.

I loved school, and the main memory I have is missing school with chicken pox when the class learned the eight and nine times tables. I never have been as secure with these two tables, so I guess my left brain needed all the help it could get!

After much coaxing, I persuaded my mother to write down some of her childhood experiences. She had just regained her eyesight after cataract and lens implant operations. To her, this was a miracle, to be able to write again. The tales she recorded were so charming, I felt sad I hadn't been able to cajole her into writing much more. She was very articulate and an entertaining storyteller. Our family enjoyed Mother's writing so much, I thought I should write down my recollections while I was able. As a result, I got busy writing my own memoirs. It was a lot of fun and interesting to discover that when we start searching our memories, the recall of certain events would trigger memories of others. When we have been at it awhile, events long forgotten will come back in great detail. Many times ..on't be able to pinpoint when an event occurred at first, but gradually, it will come into focus.

There are interesting events in all our lives, even though we might think our own lives could not be all that interesting. I highly recommend recording the events of your life for your descendants. These remembrances are usually treasured.

To get started, do your writing as though you are talking or writing a letter to someone you know well. Something as personal as your recollections can be a valuable peek at earlier years for your descendants. You will derive much pleasure from the experience of recalling the times of your life. If you are unable or unwilling to write, experiment with a tape recorder. It may feel awkward at first, but after you become accustomed to talking into a machine, you will find it quite enjoyable. It will probably help to have someone ask you questions at first. Jot down some notes to guide you; organize them as you go along or wait until later, whatever works. Have fun and bon voyage!

> *"Every action of our lives*
> *touches some chord*
> *that will vibrate in eternity."*
> —E.H. Chapin

December 24. What Do We Tell Ourselves?

We've all heard about self-fulfilling prophecies, but do we recognize how often we set ourselves up for pre-determined results? I find myself thinking more and more about subjects such as acceptance and change, as in the Serenity Prayer:

*"Grant me the serenity to accept
the things I cannot change,
the courage to change the things I can,
and the wisdom to know the difference."*

The kicker is in that last phrase: to be able to know the difference between what we can change and what we cannot change. We often blame events or people for getting us upset. Those things can't upset us unless we give them permission to do so. Once you become aware you have this power, you can change your reaction and refuse to let yourself be controlled by situations and other people. Most of your feelings and the ways you react to events have become habitual over your lifetime. If you find they are neither productive nor effective, this becomes something you can change. You may not be able to control getting upset at all times, but you do have a lot of control over how upset you will be.

Unlearning a habit can be very uncomfortable. Try clasping your hands with the opposite thumb on top. It feels very awkward. If you want to unlearn an old habit, it is easier if you replace it with a new one you like better.

We all had dreams and expectations of how we would like our lives to go. When they don't turn out that way, we can usually regroup and go forward. In a stressful situation, we can recognize the source of the stress if we think about it. Most problems are not as impossible as we make them seem. They can be unfortunate, sad or embarrassing, but not impossible.

*"If there is no solution,
there is no problem."*

Think about that statement. How many times have you stressed yourself seeking a solution for things over which you had absolutely no control? Acceptance is what you seek in such cases, and you must tell yourself when to let go.

Most of the time we are our own harshest critics. We are told not to judge ourselves so stringently, but there are times we find we are doing that by the way we talk to ourselves. Even with all our perceived shortcomings, we usually manage to accept ourselves to a degree, but there are circumstances when we hear self-judgement pop up again. To have others accept us as we are, we owe it to ourselves to like what we are.

Listen to what you say to yourself and see if you can observe how it affects your reactions. Tell yourself what you want to hear and be. I have found, in the long run, things will pretty well even out. When you look back you can sense how differently you look at things compared to years ago. Practice sending yourself positive messages throughout your day whenever you doubt yourself. You are a wise, confident person who is able to make wise decisions!

*"The farther backward you can look,
the farther forward you will be able to see"*
—Winston Churchill

December 31. Re-examine Goals

When the new year turns, we face evaluating our past performance. I often count on friends or circumstances to suggest new ideas, but everyone is rushing around, caught up in the hustle of the season. I think about the ways we set some goals for ourselves, and I wonder how many we actually reach or even start. I found a good quote: "Everyone has problems. Just make sure you don't have the same ones every year."

Look over the goals you set for yourself last year. Which resolutions were achieved? Which one did you make some progress toward? Success may be defined this way: "The progressive realization of a worthy goal." Notice, it doesn't specify *reaching* the goal, but *progressing toward it*.

Which of last year's goals have you learned to overcome or deal with? Have you discovered any new ones, or are they the same old ones you have had on your mind for many years? If they are still the same, perhaps you overestimated your ability and need to be more realistic. Success depends on the presence of two precepts: 1) you feel your life will be better for it; 2) you sincerely believe you can accomplish the task. There may be a lot of one without the other, but without both, success is likely to be elusive.

It is not as hopeless as it sounds. If you have not been successful in reaching or making progress toward your desired goals, it is time to take a look at them. Break each goal into smaller steps, ones which you are confident you can reach. In some cases, the goals may have ceased to be important to you. Many times when you feel you have failed, you have merely taken on too big a job at once. Planning for more manageable, small goals will give you a chance to succeed along the longer path.

It is a good thing to have a goal to work toward, no matter how small. If you don't move forward in some way, it is easy to become stagnant. You must map out the actions you will have to take to achieve your short term goals, such as a date when you will go to a class, write those letters, or read that book. To make progress, you do have to be specific. Otherwise, it is easy to let things slide once more.

Before you make your New Year's resolutions, re-evaluate from past years, then *get real*.

"The way to do things is to begin!"
—Horace Greeley

Appendix A. Birthday Bonus

Extra Special

THINKING BACK OVER YOUR LIFE, whom would you name as the first person, besides a family member, who made you feel special? For some of us, perhaps these special people were the first ones, period!

We hear a lot these days about how much influence the way we were treated when we were young has on our future relationships. I was fortunate to have had a very supportive family, and I received encouragement in most of my undertakings. The first person outside my family to offer that special encouragement was an art instructor with whom I studied at age fourteen. The fact that he wasn't from my family gave me an entirely different feeling of achievement.

Teachers are very high on this list for many of us. These skilled and dedicated people deserve appreciation for inspiring their students to broaden their horizons and reach for the stars. As you think back to that first person who gave you a feeling of being special, consider how important that was to you. These recollections may prompt you to do two things: 1) thank that person who encouraged you, if he or she is still accessible; and 2) resolve to encourage a child in like manner.

Once you are grown, of course, no matter what your childhood was like, you must take hold of your life and make it what you want it to be. It is another example of how your attitude makes all the difference. Looking at your life positively, you can choose to act as though you are the person you want to be. Pretty soon you will find that you *are* what you want to be, or at least have a better idea of just what that is.

As parents or teachers ourselves, we all do the best we know how to do at a given time. We may realize we fell short sometimes, and we probably did. We have to learn to forgive our families and others when they didn't fulfill our needs.

Maybe you fell short of your own expectations. It is essential to forgive yourself as well, and go ahead with being the best you can be. There is still time.

> *"Forgiveness is the fragrance*
> *the violet sheds*
> *on the heel that crushed it."*

Appendix B.
Special Observations for Caregivers

A Reading for Spring. Caregivers

WHO OR WHAT IS A CAREGIVER? One definition is a person who has principal care for an ill family member. In the larger sense, any good friend or family member may become a caregiver.

Our first concerns are for the ill person, who certainly needs loving thoughts. Nevertheless, when we analyze the situation, the patient is usually receiving medical care and, often, eventually becomes quite content and worry-free. If there is pain or anxiety, further medical help is usually possible.

When the ill person is being cared for in the home, the caregiver struggles with the emotional feelings engendered by the role reversal taking place, being overwhelmed by the added responsibilities, along with concern for the patient.

There is a surprisingly difficult adjustment when an aging parent and an adult child exchange roles, but even more when it is a spouse one must care for. Not everyone is a natural nurse. There are still all the stages of loss to go through: denial, anger, grief and, finally, acceptance.

We find friends and family members to be exceedingly concerned about the patient, but only the most perceptive are aware of the stress upon the well person.

If you are the caregiver, you are likely to go through periods of "awfulizing," projecting all the dire things ahead. You wonder if you are capable of meeting the challenges of the added responsibilities.

The caregiver, little by little, has to take over tasks formerly handled by the patient. When that time came for me, I was most grateful that my husband had always insisted we share financial decisions and policies, even doing income taxes together. It made my transition in these areas less stressful.

When it becomes apparent that you must take on the unfamiliar added responsibilities, it is likely you will find that no matter how well you believe you have accepted the situation, you must work through the process again whenever there is a change. You must work through the loss of your companion or parent as you have known them and adjust to this new person. You become *their* security blanket, their link to reality. Many of the problems can best be solved with love, since the patient is very tuned into your moods and usually responds in kind.

Many of us are surprised to find our patience is not as good as we once thought, and we suffer great guilt at being impatient with someone who has little or no control over their behavior. We place superhuman expectations on ourselves and hope no one ever discovers this new self we are ashamed of.

Support groups are now widely available; they can help reassure you that you are not alone.

Having a place where people will listen to your concerns without judgment and will share coping skills will give you additional courage to hang in there.

If you find yourself in a caregiver's role, learn to live for—and deal with—one day at a time. And learn to love and care for yourself. You can't be much help as a caregiver if you, as the caregiver, get sick. To help yourself keep well and better able to handle your new tasks:

- Find quality time to be with friends.
- Follow a hobby.
- Get plenty of exercise and rest.
- Eat nutritious meals.
- Maintain your relationship with God.
- Know when it's time to get help for your own sake.

We don't have to wait until we are in a caregiving role to communicate our support to principle caregivers. We can benefit from the following quote:

> "What life means to us is determined not so much by what life brings us, as by what attitude we bring to life; not so much by what happens to us as by our reaction to what happens."
>
> —Lewis L. Dunnington

A Reading for Summer. Middle Distance

When I was feeling more harried than usual, a good friend said I needed to relax and look at the "middle distance." When I inquired what that was, she said I would have to figure it out myself. As I tried to crystallize my thoughts concerning that admonition, I came to some conclusions I believe worth passing along.

There is looking back, and there is looking forward. Perhaps where we need to look is in the *now*. When my husband had to move out of the apartment we shared to the nursing component of our retirement community, I was no longer part of a couple. Nor was I single. That had become apparent long before he moved, since there had not been any two-way conversations for several years. Even so, I missed that warm body near me, although I could no longer manage his care. His loving arms had taken care of a lot of challenges.

After he moved, trying to take him to some of his favorite places served only to confuse him, and once he had become adjusted, he felt more comfortable when left to following the routine of the nursing pavilion. For memory-impaired people, having to make decisions, not adhering to a set routine, leads to anxiety. It became clear that taking him places was an activity that benefited me, rather than him. Trying to bring back the past only confused him.

I wondered if my postponing the decision to move him to the nursing pavilion actually postponed his receiving needed care. When the time comes that we can no longer cope, our loved ones are usually so tuned in to our moods, they probably are affected by our being overwhelmed. The difficulty is that they are not able to understand our separation; that is the worst part!

An impaired person definitely lives in the *now*. That's all that's left. Recent memory is usually the first to go, then the long-term memory gets hazy and finally disappears. It is difficult to imagine how it must feel to have only *now*.

For me, the past is good for reminiscing, but not for regrets. Future is good for planning, but not for worry. All we really have to deal with most of the time is *now*. I came to the conclusion that *now* is my "middle distance." Perhaps yours is in a different place. Indeed, mine may be different another day.

"Today is the tomorrow you worried about yesterday!"

A Reading for Autumn. Neither Single Nor a Couple

WHEN YOU HAVE BEEN CARING FOR A SPOUSE with a chronic impairment, at some point you realize that you are not often socializing as a couple any more. On the other hand, you do not have the freedom to make or reinforce single friendships, nor become involved in previous, pleasurable activities.

Studies have shown that for good mental health, we all need to spend a major part of our day in activities we enjoy. In a caregiving situation, can we say we often have that choice? We learn to cope with the various challenges as we go along.

At some point we recognize we need help in keeping ourselves healthy and able to cope with the caregiving. Our doctors will tell us how important it is to build some activities and friendships for ourselves. The couples we know well who do still include us in appropriate social events are much appreciated for their understanding. When my husband became unable to cope with many social activities, I began to let a great number of my outside activities go, not consciously, but by being too fatigued to make the effort.

We learn to cope with the various challenges we face as we go along. Anyone in this position comes to understand what a virtue patience is and how hard it is to maintain. There are many books to helps us, as well as support groups. Knowing others in the same position who share their experiences is most helpful, and it helps us to understand we are not alone. In such groups we find that each patient reacts a little differently because of his or her prior life experiences.

It is necessary to branch out and reinforce friendships with both old and new friends. We find we miss the company and conversation of others. (Most dementia people are not great conversationalists!) We do have to take the initiative to be with other people more. Many of us tend to stay with our impaired spouse too much, when it is important to have the company and conversation of others, to maintain a much-needed balance in our lives.

There are community facilities for adult day care, listed in most phone books under "Social Services," for those unable to hire outside help.

Eventually we need to build a different kind of recreation for ourselves. If we wait too long, it might be too late. I have known many caregivers whose own health, both emotional and physical, suffered irreparably.

We can still play the important role of being part of a couple, as the security for our spouse. Nonetheless, we must find activities that will take us out of ourselves for limited periods. I'm sure some guilt will creep in when we think about going out and enjoying ourselves, but if we get completely worn down, how much good will we be to anyone, ourselves included?

You may get good advice from professionals, but sometimes it takes experience to fully understand what they are talking about. Stay part of that important couple, but don't neglect yourself. You are not obliged to be Superspouse-Nurse-Caregiver in order to do this job well. You do have to balance your life, and perhaps you will have to think back to remember how to do that!

Being good to yourself is not selfish, but prudent, if you want to continue to be that loving caregiver.

*"Even if you are on the right track,
you will get run over if you just sit there!"*

A Reading for Winter. Survivors

WHAT IS A SURVIVOR, and how does one get that way? By putting one foot in front of another! By continuing to paddle, even against the current! Perhaps you didn't think too much about the subject until you were faced with solving a difficult challenge in your life.

Much of the time our lives go along on fairly predictable paths. It isn't until we face something we had never considered before that we discover whether we are survivors. I recently saw a report of a study on children in urban ghettos. The children were followed for many years to see if there was some factor that enabled some of them to survive in spite of their backgrounds and poverty. The children who were able to maintain a good sense of self, even if they did not get reinforcement from their families, were most likely to come out of this background with their heads on straight.

In a course on "What makes people tick?" the teacher spoke of the origin of self-esteem. Our genes make a contribution. The way our parents acted or taught us also has an impact. Sometimes the opposite of what our parents said and did has an effect. The instructor told us we are victims of the way we *perceive* or *experience* an event, not of the event itself.

It is a natural thing for our bodies and minds to want to maintain internal stability, and we usually arrange our environment (anything outside our body envelope) to accomplish this. We have something called the "General Adaptation Syndrome," which automatically kicks in when it senses stress. It can't distinguish good stress from bad stress. Stress comes in many forms; it can be a first date or a driver's test. The physical effects are the same. Our bodies will react with anxiety or we will adapt. Our behavior is a result of our *reaction*, not the event. It is the way we experience or perceive these events that determines if it is good or bad stress.

It sounds as though our perceptions have a lot to do with the way we become survivors. Does this have anything to do with being an optimist or a pessimist? Does this doom those of us who find ourselves pessimistic? Not necessarily. Changing the way we view an event can be accomplished by deciding we can do it. That sounds easy, but it isn't.

Repeat to yourself throughout the day the messages you want to develop. Write the messages to yourself and post them where you can see them. This will go far in helping you change your perceptions. You can't always control the events in your life, but you can decide how you will react to them, physically or emotionally. Survivors are the ones who learn from every experience, find answers and go on.

Being a caregiver for an impaired spouse, I found when emotions were involved, the stress of this job exacted a tremendous toll on my health. I have not always been the kind, patient caregiver I would wish to be. In fact, I don't know too many angels! To be a survivor, we have to consider being kind and accepting of ourselves, as well as of the one we care for. All of us have felt discouraged or overwhelmed at times. This is part of living. We often feel we have to have the solution to every problem, monumental or small, and until we admit this is not possible, we can't get on with our job.

Some of our distress comes from anger, guilt or helplessness, and we pray for patience and strength to do what we must do. Many times it comes down to accepting ourselves and our limitations. Isolating which problems are not our responsibility is often as hard as finding solutions. Therefore, it appears survivors are both born and made!

At some point, we have to let go and let God. Hang in there, survivors!

> *"Life is easier than you think. All you have to do is accept the impossible, do without the indispensable, and bear the intolerable."*